THE MISHNAIC LAW OF BLESSINGS AND PRAYERS

Program in Judaic Studies
Brown University
BROWN JUDAIC STUDIES
Edited by
Jacob Neusner,
Wendell S. Dietrich, William Scott Green, Ernest S. Frerichs,
Calvin Goldscheider, Alan Zuckerman

Project Editors (Project)

David Blumenthal, Emory University (Approaches to Medieval Judaism)
William Brinner (Studies in Judaism and Islam)
Ernest S. Frerichs, Brown University (Dissertations and Monographs)
Lenn Evan Goodman, University of Hawaii (Studies in Medieval Judaism)
(Studies in Judaism and Islam)
William Scott Green, University of Rochester (Approaches to Ancient
Judaism)
Ivan Marcus, Jewish Theological Seminary of America
(Texts and Studies in Medieval Judaism)
Marc L. Raphael, Ohio State University (Approaches to Judaism in
Modern Times)
Norbert Samuelson, Temple University (Jewish Philosophy)
Jonathan Z. Smith, University of Chicago (Studia Philonica)

Number 88
THE MISHNAIC LAW OF BLESSINGS AND PRAYERS
Tractate Berakhot

by
Tzvee Zahavy

THE MISHNAIC LAW OF BLESSINGS AND PRAYERS

Tractate Berakhot

by
Tzvee Zahavy

Scholars Press
Atlanta, Georgia

THE MISHNAIC LAW OF BLESSINGS AND PRAYERS
Tractate Berakhot

Copyright © 1987 by Brown University

Paperback edition published 2007 by Brown Judaic Studies

Library of Congress Cataloging-in-Publication Data

Zahavy, Tzvee.
      The Mishnaic law of blessings and prayers.

      (Brown Judaic Studies ; no. 88)
      Includes translation of Mishnah Berakhot and selections from Tosefta Berakhot with commentary.
      Bibliography: p.
      Includes index.
      1. Mishnah. Berakhot—Commentaries. 2. Tosefta. Berakhot—Commentaries. 3. Judaism—Liturgy. I. Mishnah. Berakhot. English. 1987. II. Tosefta. Berakhot. English. Selections. 1987. III. Title. IV. Series.

BM506.B63Z34   1987   296.1'2307   87-4868
ISBN 1-55540-120-1 (alk. paper ; cloth)
ISBN 978-1-930675-45-2 (alk paper ; paper)

Printed in the United States of America
on acid-free paper

מוקדש לכבוד

יום הולדתו החמישים וחמש

של רבי

יעקב בן שמואל הכהן נוסנר

איש ספר

מורה דורנו

CONTENTS

Preface

I started this research intending to study tractates Mishnah and Tosefta Berakhot to contribute to the understanding of the character of the early rabbinic compilations Mishnah and Tosefta. At the time that I began the work, my teacher, Professor Jacob Neusner of Brown University, was completing a major study of many of the other tractates of Mishnah and Tosefta.[1] I undertook this work at first as a study parallel to his: as a systematic investigation of the nature of the forms and contents of the texts of tractate Berakhot of Mishnah and Tosefta.

As my research unfolded, I found that my analysis of this one tractate for the purposes established by Neusner in his work confirmed most of the conclusions he reached in his study of other parts of Mishnah and Tosefta. In the early stages of my work, I observed first of all that there were few new literary forms or formulary patterns in my tractate. I therefore chose not to undertake what would be repetitive studies of Mishnaic diction in Berakhot.

I saw in addition that, by and large, the substantive characteristics of M. and T. described by Neusner in his studies of other tractates also reverberated in the present texts. Most striking was my confirmation of Neusner's insight into the substantive coherence of the content of each chapter of Mishnah.[2] In Berakhot at first there does not appear to be much of a coherent agendum of issues in each redactional unit of the tractate. But based on Neusner's consistent findings for the remainder of Mishnah, I ferreted out the major interest or concern of each chapter and was able to delineate the themes which lend coherence to Mishnah's sometimes ostensibly disparate rules. In the introduction to each chapter of this book I present the results of this analysis.

My primary goal remained to provide insight into the character of the texts of Mishnah and Tosefta in their larger textual contexts. Based on my study of Berakhot, I concluded that an issue specific to this tractate also had to be addressed. These M. and T. texts inform us about early rabbinic conceptions of prayer and blessings, of the daily liturgy, and of table fellowship. No past systematic analyses of these texts had attended closely enough to what these

---

[1]These studies have been published in the series *Studies in Judaism in Late Antiquity*. They include *A History of the Mishnaic Law of Purities, A History of the Mishnaic Law of Holy Things, A History of the Mishnaic Law of Damages, A History of the Mishnaic Law of Women, A History of the Mishnaic Law of Appointed Times* (Leiden: E.J. Brill).

[2]This is summarized in the introduction to each of the tractates in the individual studies in SJLA and somewhat recapitulated in *Judaism: The Evidence of Mishnah* (Chicago: 1981).

corpora of texts *on their own* had to say about these matters. Accordingly, I decided as one purpose of the present study to take a direct interest in what the data said about early Jewish ritual, to investigate issues relating to the nature and development of early rabbinic conceptions of blessings, prayer, and table fellowship.

This book is addressed to a broad audience of specialists. Because the central purpose of this work is to make a contribution to the study of Jewish life and thought in late antiquity from the first through third centuries C.E., I expect that this book will serve the interests of historians of ancient Judaism, of Mishnaic and Talmudic religious law, and of the development of Jewish liturgy.

The contents of this book relate to many aspects of Jewish cultural development in that formative period. Students of Hellenistic history and religion and of early Christianity also may find information of interest in this study because Judaic religious practices and beliefs reflect and influence parallel developments in other related social and cultural contexts in antiquity.

Others also may find information of value in this book. It is commonly assumed that during the time of the formation and redaction of Mishnah, from the first through the third centuries, the rabbis instituted many forms of prayer and blessings, and articulated formative philosophical understandings of prayer which influenced the development of Jewish and Christian prayer for centuries to follow. Knowledge of the character of earliest rabbinic liturgy may be useful to all those who wish to trace the development of subsequent forms of Western prayer.

Finally, this study may contribute modestly to the understanding of prayer in general. Historians of religion, scholars of comparative religious thought and practice, phenomenologists of religion, anthropologists who study religious ritual, and sociologists of religion, may find in this analysis of a formative corpus of textual data, some small methodological and substantive advances for the study of prayer and similar rituals in the contexts of other religions of the world.

Acknowledgements

I thank the College of Liberal Arts and the Graduate School of the University of Minnesota for numerous grants and research leaves which supported parts of this project. The American Council of Learned Societies awarded me a fellowship in 1983 to work on research related to this book. I also thank the dean of the Faculty of the Humanities of the Hebrew University for his assistance in providing for me an office and access to the libraries during my tenure there as Visiting Scholar in the Winter and Spring of 1983 as I completed this study.

Above all I acknowledge the influence on this study of the work of my teacher, Jacob Neusner. He has shown us all how to render the wisdom of our sages into our own language through his own lucid and systematic work in his translations and explanations of tractates of the Mishnah, the Tosefta, the Talmud of the Land of Israel, the Babylonian Talmud, the Midrash, and in his ongoing work on the remaining documents of rabbinic literature. I am grateful for what he has given me to work with. I know that without the benefit of Neusner's paradigmatic work, my translation and study of Mishnah and Tosefta Berakhot could not have succeeded in whatever small measure it has.

Introduction

I. Blessings and Prayers:
The Message of Tractate Berakhot

A. Background

The few brief and turbulent generations between the years 70 and 200 of the common era were revolutionary times in the development of religion in the ancient near East. One of the most dramatic and distinctive changes in the nature of religion during this period was the demise of cultic worship through animal sacrifices and agricultural offerings at centralized national shrines and the concomitant shift to worship through routinized local prayer and table fellowship.

In Judaism the change came abruptly. Prior to 70 C.E. the Temple in Jerusalem dominated Jewish worship. To serve God from day to day and throughout the year, one could participate in the rituals of the Temple as carried on by the priests in Jerusalem. When the Roman legions destroyed the Temple, the Jews looked to other modes of worship to take the place of the Temple's sacrificial cult.

Two particular changes are noteworthy in this epoch. First, in the years following the destruction of the religious center of Judaism in Jerusalem, from 70 to 132, Jews developed the practice of reciting prayers on a regular basis in their towns and villages. Second, the rites of table fellowship in each Jewish home took on a much greater significance during this era of instability and change.

In the next generation, after the abortive revolt of 132-5 C.E., when it was clear that the Temple would not speedily be rebuilt and its cult would not quickly be restored, rabbinic leaders developed these newly emphasized rituals of prayer and table fellowship as the primary means of systematic worship within the way of life they articulated in Mishnah and its appendix, Tosefta, the formulaic traditions of the rabbinic academy.

The tractates Berakhot in Mishnah and Tosefta are collections of these rabbinic rules for worship and commensality, assembled and edited in the early third century C.E. The religious laws in these collections are the best source of evidence for reconstructing the history of the development of modes and theories of rabbinic prayer and table fellowship in the era of great transition and change from the first through the third centuries.

B. The Message of the Tractate

M. Berakhot appears at first to be a somewhat disjointed tractate comprised of disparate units on a variety of loosely related topics. M.'s laws deal with the recitation of the *Shema,* the recitation of the Prayer of Eighteen Blessings, blessings to be recited before one eats foods, the common recitation of blessings after the meal, other rules for the dinner, and blessings for other occasions.

On first analysis one common concern lends coherence to the diverse laws and rules of the tractate. That basic unifying principle is that a person must recite one or more formulaic blessings in each instance of religious ritual mentioned in the tractate. Hence the title: "Berakhot," "Blessings."[1]

Accordingly, M. rules that before and after the daily recitations of the biblical verses which comprise the *Shema,* one recites blessings. For daily prayers, one recites a liturgies of eighteen blessings. At meals, one recites blessings before and after eating any foods. In times of danger, or when one obtains new clothes, or when one hears good news, or when one comes into a town from a trip abroad, or in a number of other instances, one recites blessings.

In the Mishnaic conception, the requirement to recite a common formula connects together a variety of clearly distinct religious rituals and personal or social occasions. Hence the various rules of the tractate and their subjects seem to cohere only on a superficial secondary level.

On further investigation it becomes evident that M. actually weaves together a carefully selected group of formulaic rules on related topics to construct and articulate a fully-developed and more coherent theory of prayer which carefully defines the nature of many aspects of the larger phenomenon of its concern–the recitation of the standardized literary formulae of rabbinic prayer.

A principle assumption of Mishnah Berakhot is the notion that blessings are performative utterances–words which a person recites to accomplish something of religious significance–either to transform ordinary activities into special moments of ritual, or take on an independent ritual life themselves. Blessings before and after eating, for example, alter the nature of the act of eating. They transform the meal from a mere biological act of eating to a moment of ritual sanctity.

The *Shema*-liturgies, recited early in the morning and at night, serve to frame the activity of everyday life in sanctity. Blessings before and after the *Shema* frame the recitation of biblical verses with an outline of rabbinic actions

---

[1]A blessing is a fixed array of words which first invoke God's name and then close with an appropriate formula for the specific application of the blessing. Several examples help illustrate the use of blessings in the rabbinic system. Before reciting the evening *Shema* one recites a short liturgy which concludes with a blessing, "Blessed art thou O Lord Our God, King of the Universe who brings the evening." Before eating fruit one must recite, "Blessed art thou...who creates the fruit of the tree." At the conclusion of the Sabbath one recites a liturgy which takes the form of a blessing: "Blessed art thou...who divides the sacred from the profane...."

and words and provides an interpretive framework for the traditional recitation of Scriptural selections.

Likewise other liturgical rituals such as the *Qiddush*, the Prayer of Sanctification at the beginning of the Sabbath, and the *Habdalah*, the Prayer of Division at the end of the Sabbath, frame with sanctity both the meals of the inauguration and conclusion of the Sabbath and the Sabbath day itself. In sum, the proper words transform ordinary actions or periods of time into holy occasions, says Mishnah.

Mishnah also teaches that blessings may take on an independent existence, apart from other rituals. The recitation of the Prayer of Eighteen, for example, constitutes an autonomous ritual, with its own religious significance. Other blessings by themselves may sanctify time or action, and also may protect an individual from harm or may express an individual's thanksgiving for God's protection and grace.

Curiously, within this tractate one finds few restrictions on the location acceptable for reciting prayers and blessings. Contrary to one's expectations, the institution of the synagogue does not serve as a central setting in this compilation for the recitation of the liturgies and prayers of the late antique Israelite. The laws themselves govern actions which may be performed throughout the village, in houses, streets, marketplaces, groves, vineyards, near latrines, in bathhouses, and in synagogues and study halls as well.

We may conclude accordingly, that the rabbis believed that through the recitation of prayers with proper intention and action an ordinary householder transforms his locale, wherever that may be, into a place of sanctity. He brings the sacred into his house and village by reciting the right words, with the correct intentions, at the proper time, under the appropriate circumstances.

The tractate begins appropriately with laws for the recitation of the *Shema*. The central components of the *Shema*, verses from Deuteronomy, distinctly affirm the obligations of the individual Israelite in his village. He must love God, take God's words into his heart, and teach his children. The verses of the *Shema* in Scripture speak of places and times in the domain of the ordinary life of each person, from the doorpost of one's house to the village gates. The biblical passage alludes to the span of the typical day, from rising in the morning to retiring at night. The main obligations set forth in this section of Scripture relate to the normal existence of the individual householder. Each adult male must wear on his person tefillin and fringes. On the doorposts of each family's house there must be a mezuzah.

In short, the *Shema*-ritual is a paradigm of rabbinic religious practice. Mishnah Berakhot as its main task sets forth the basic rules for this and several other major rituals of rabbinic daily life, with a distinctive message imbedded in the rules of the Tractate. Words only become effective sacred utterances of speech, i.e. prayers and blessings, when properly uttered according to the principles set forth by the rabbis.

C. The Tractate's Systematic Definition of Prayer and Its Key Issues

The tractate as a coherent entity, in its substantive selection and organization of early rabbinic rules for liturgical recitations, enunciates a clear, structured early rabbinic definition of prayer utilizing three broad major concepts and numerous subsidiary ideas. The basic distinctions in M. are:

(1) There are two types of prayers. The first type, independent, primary prayers and blessings, constitute the main elements of a ritual. The other kind, dependent secondary prayers and blessings, serve as subsidiary adjuncts to other rituals.

(2) Second, and related to the preceding idea, the texts of prayers are often either framed by accompanying materials or serve as frames for other rituals.

(3) Prayers are comprised of at least two elements: a verbal and a mental component, i.e. an act of recitation and a state of concentration.

1. Types of Prayers

To understand the first part of M.'s definition, let us consider how M. broadly organizes the material in this tractate.

In the first half of the tractate, chapters one through five, M. deals with those prayers which stand on their own as independent rituals–the daily liturgies of rabbinic Judaism. Throughout the first five chapters of the tractate M. presents rules which regulate the rituals of the recitation of the texts of the *Shema* and of the blessings which comprise the Prayer of Eighteen.

In the second part of the tractate, chapters six through nine, M. takes up the rules for those prayers and blessings which serve as secondary elements of other rituals, first turning to regulations for the recitation of those blessings which accompany the meal. In actuality, the meals themselves are the focal rituals. The blessings merely frame the meal and establish it as a ritual occasion. Berakhot's laws propose that only through the recitation of the correct formulae before and after the meal, can one define a situation of eating as a fellowship dinner (chapters 6 and 7).

The concluding section, chapter nine, spells out other secondary prayers and blessings–those one recites for special events. One says certain formulae to give thanks to God for deliverance from danger, to request protection from harm, or to recognize the national or historical importance of a place, or the significance of an unusual natural event (ch. 9). These blessings have no function if they are recited detached from the events with which Mishnah connects them.

Accordingly, in Mishnah Berakhot's view there are two related but distinct kinds of prayers. There are those independent prayers, such as the *Shema* or the

Prayer of Eighteen, which one recites apart from of any other focal event or ritual. Next, there are those dependent blessings recited over foods or at various times which are adjuncts to other actions.

2. *Framing Prayers*

Mishnah's second implicit interpretive concept is the idea that some rituals need to be formally framed or demarcated. The rabbinic meal is one example of a ritual framed by the recitation of blessings. Blessings before and after eating transform acts of consuming food, which they surround, into sacred occasions of ritual (cf. M. Chapters 6 and 7). The rabbinic blessings recited before and after the scriptural passages of the *Shema* (see M. 1:4) serve to frame the recitation of these verses from the Torah, and transform the act from mere speech or study into liturgy. M.'s perception is that some rituals may be framed through the recitation of the formulae of prayers or blessings, and that some prayers themselves may be framed by other liturgical devices.

Visible, but less urgent concerns of this tractate of Mishnah are such notions that prayers and other rituals may be differentiated from ordinary activities in a variety of ways, not just through the recitation of other preliminary and concluding formulary texts. Physical signals such as posture, tone of voice, demeanor, dress, or the use of special objects, serve a similar purpose. In addition the physical locale or the social context of a prayer or another ritual may set it off from the profane endeavors of everyday life.

3. *Intention for Reciting Blessings and Prayers*

M. expresses its third fundamental notion of its definition of prayer in a few choice rules governing the recitation of the liturgies. In order for an individual to properly recite the *Shema*, M. requires that one achieve a certain level of concentration which shuts out some of the ordinary interactions of social life (M. 2:1). Likewise for the correct recitation of the Prayer of Eighteen, one must completely close out the distractions of the physical world and turn his attention inward, to prayer (M. 5:1). In addition Mishnah emphasizes that special positive forms of intention or concentration must accompany the recitation of prayers.

4. *Subsidiary Ideas*

a. Framing the Daily Cycle

Several subsidiary notions of prayers and blessings inhere in the remaining rules of the tractate. In Mishnah's view, the *Shema* and the Prayer of Eighteen play a role in demarcating the structure of daily life. The *Shema* marks the beginning and end of every day (M. 1:1-3). The blessings which frame the *Shema* express many of the rabbinic beliefs concerning the nature of the daily cycle of life and the importance and purpose of a person's daily endeavors.

The liturgical texts (blessings) which frame the morning *Shema*, make mention of God's role in the creation of light and darkness and in renewing each day his acts of creation of the world. They refer to the basic rabbinic beliefs in the revelation of the Torah, in redemption, and salvation. The blessings surrounding the evening *Shema* make reference to God's role in bringing the darkness of night, his love for his people Israel, his promise for the redemption of the people. In this liturgy one asks for God's protection through the night to come.

Each Jew recites the blessings of the Prayer of Eighteen and invokes many of the important beliefs of rabbinism to mark the cycle of each passing day, morning, afternoon, and night.

b.   Intention: Subsidiary Ideas

Earlier I said that M. requires intention or concentration for the recitation of prayers. Several rules in this tractate add conceptions subsidiary to this fundamental notion. For example, M. recognizes that the social realities of the pressures of a person's daily life may affect an individual's ability to concentrate for prayer. M. exempts from the obligation to recite the *Shema*, a newlywed who cannot properly concentrate because he is emotionally distracted (M. 2:5). In addition the text recognizes the limitations of a mourner's ability to achieve the proper frame of mind for prayer because of his grief (M. 3:1-2).

M. further rules that a craftsman may recite the *Shema* while atop a tree (M. 2:4). An ordinary householder cannot because he will not be able to properly concentrate while high above the ground. These additional rulings develop derivative notions of how one must alter his awareness to make special efforts to concentrate during the recitation of the *Shema* and the Prayer of Eighteen.

c.   Excluded Classes and other Deficiencies in Recitation

Other rulings, also subsidiary to the main ideas of the tractate, except certain classes of individuals from the obligation to recite prayers. M. excludes women, slaves and minors, individuals who suffered a pollution, and those who stand unclothed or near waste materials (M. 3:3-6) from participation in the rituals of prayer. M. also specifies how the level of a person's voice and the correct pronunciation of the words of liturgies contribute to the proper execution of the ritual. In addition, one's posture and bodily orientation are all factors in defining and properly framing liturgical recitations (M. 2:4-6, 1:3).

d.   Food Blessings: Taxonomy and Economy

As I said, the second half of the tractate develops ideas concerning those secondary prayers which accompany other rituals–the blessings one recites before and after eating and the blessings for other special events. M. presents a simple system of those blessings to be recited before eating any foods, representing its idea of a basic taxonomy of foods. It distinguishes separate categories for bread and wine, for fruits, for vegetables, and for all other foods (M. 6:1-3).

In addition to its outline of the system of food blessings, M. spells out a second important substantive concept. One must make exceedingly sparing use of these blessings presumably because they invoke the name of God (M. 6:4-7).

To review, the chief concerns of M.'s third-century rabbinic definition of prayer in the tractate are:

1. The distinction of independent from dependent prayers.

2. How to frame the texts of prayers to separate them from ordinary speech.

3. How blessings may bracket the rituals of prayer and of the fellowship meal.

4. Various other modes of framing the act of prayer with physical signals, such as voice, posture and orientation.

5. The nature of the mental processes associated with prayer.

6. The relationship between real social structures and situations, and the theoretical demands of the recitation of prayers.

7. How blessings support conceptions of taxonomic structures of natural produce.

8. How one makes economical use of the formulae of blessings recited in the context of the meal.

The diagram (figure 1) summarizes many of the main elements of M.'s definition of prayer. (See p. 146 below.)

Now that I have spelled out the major ideas which comprise the message of Berakhot, I turn in the next section to a summary of the rules in *the order they appear in the tractate*. After that, in section III, I consider how Berakhot fits into its broader cultural context. In IV, I describe the methods of translation and commentary I use in the chapters which follow.

II. The Structure of Tractate Berakhot

Let us summarize the laws of the compilation in order. Tractate Berakhot in Mishnah begins with the rules for the recitation of the *Shema* and unfolds in seven major divisions as follows:

A. Rules for the recitation of the *Shema* and its blessings (1:1-5)

1:1   Dispute regarding the time for the recitation of the *Shema* at night.

1:2   Dispute regarding the recitation of the *Shema* in the morning.

1:3   Houses' dispute over the exegesis of Deut. 6:7. Scriptural basis for reciting evening and morning.

1:4   The rabbinic blessings which frame the *Shema*. General rules regarding forms of blessings.

1:5   Scriptural basis for reciting the last verse of the *Shema* at night.

B. Concentration during the recitation. Social status and the recitation of the *Shema* (2:1-3:6)

2:1-2   Intention needed for reciting. Distractions from reciting. The basis for the order of the paragraphs.

2:3   One who erred in reciting.

2:4   Special rule for craftsmen. May recite atop a tree. It is no distraction for them.

2:5-7   Bridegroom exempt from the *Shema*. He is distracted. Gamaliel's practice and two more units about Gamaliel.

2:8   Bridegroom has the option to recite.

3:1-2   Those involved in a funeral are exempt from the *Shema*.

3:3   Women, slaves and minors are exempt from the *Shema*. Their other obligations.

3:4   One for whom the rabbis declared uncleanness (because of a bodily discharge) may not recite the rabbinic blessings before and after the *Shema* and before the meal.

3:5   Related rules: Prayer-obligation of one who remembered he was unclean. Reciting the *Shema* while unclothed. Prayer near human wastes.

3:6   Others who are unclean from a discharge must dip in a pool before they can recite the *Shema*.

C. Rules for the recitation of the Prayer of Eighteen Blessings (4:1-5:5)

4:1   The times of day to recite the Prayer.

4:2   Special Prayers for a study hall.

4:3   Dispute regarding the Prayer of Eighteen.

4:4   Fixing Prayer. Short Prayer to be said in a place of danger.

4:5   Direction to face when praying.

4:6   One who prays when travelling.

4:7   The Additional Prayer.

5:1   The frame of mind needed for Prayer.

5:2   Insertions in the Prayer.

5:3   Rules for one who makes errors in praying.

5:4   The priestly blessing during Prayer.

5:5   Prayer recitation as an omen.

D. Rules for food blessings and the blessings of the meal and dinner (6:1-8)

6:1 The basic taxonomy of categories of foods and their respective blessings.

6:2 Reciting the wrong blessing.

6:3 Blessings over non-agricultural or defective foods.

6:4 Priorities of foods for reciting blessings.

6:5 Reciting a blessing over one food exempts another from the need for a blessing.

6:6 One person's blessing exempts another person from the obligation to recite a blessing.

6:7 Primary and secondary foods in the meal.

6:8 The blessings recited after eating. The blessing for drinking water.

E. The invitation to recite the blessings after a meal (7:1-5)

7:1-2 The call to recite the blessings after the meal. Who may be counted in the necessary quorum.

7:3 The formula of the invitation.

7:4-5 How a group may separate or combine for the invitation. The blessing over wine.

F. Dinner rituals (8:1-8)

8:1 Houses' disputes regarding the dinner. The order of blessings in the Sabbath Prayer of Sanctification (Qiddush).

8:2 The order of washing and mixing the cup at dinner.

8:3 Placement of the napkin at the dinner.

8:4 Cleaning and washing after the dinner.

8:5 The order of blessings in the Prayer of Division (Habdalah) after the Sabbath.

8:6 The blessings over light and spices after the meal.

8:7 Rule for one who forgot to recite the blessings after the meal.

8:8 Blessings on wine and meal after dinner.

G. Other blessings and miscellaneous matters (9:1-5)

9:1 Blessings for shrines and former places of idolatry.

9:2 Blessings for astronomical, geological and meteorological phenomena.

9:3 Blessings to recite when acquiring new possessions or for hearing good or bad news. Vain Prayers.

9:4   Prayers to recite upon entering a new town.

9:5   Blessings to recite for good and bad events. Proper behavior at the Temple Mount. The rabbis ordained the invocation of God's name.

To sum up, A and B cover the nature of the obligation to recite the *Shema* morning and evening (1:1-5); intention which is needed for reciting the *Shema* and the kinds of distractions which disrupt the recitation of the *Shema* (2:1-3:2). This material ends with rules for individuals who are not obliged to recite the *Shema* or its blessings (3:3-6).

C turns to the second daily liturgy, the Prayer, and deals with: the times (4:1) and forms of the Prayer (4:3-4), one's orientation during Prayer (4:5-6), the Additional Prayer (4:7). Interpolations into this Mishnaic unit deal with the short special Prayer for the study hall and for places of danger (4:2, 4:4). It turns then to the frame of mind one needs for the Prayer (5:1) and to other regulations.

D covers food blessings (6:1-7), E addresses the blessings after the meal (6:8, 7:1-5) and F deals with dinner regulations (8:1-8). G concludes with rules for special blessings.

As I said, on the whole the Mishnah-tractate does not evince substantive conceptual internal coherence. Its unity grows out of the perspective of the editor who brought together a variety of subjects which share in common the practice of the recitation of the rabbinic blessing formula in each of these instances of daily activity.

III. Mishnah in its Larger Cultural Settings: The Contexts of Tractate Berakhot

A. Scriptural Context of the Tractate

The system of blessings and prayers described in this tractate is based mainly on rabbinic innovation and invention. The rabbis constructed this elaborate compilation of rules with only a slim foundation of Scriptural allusions to prayers and blessings or of any regulations for the rituals of prayer.

The text of the liturgy itself is built out of an interweaving of citations and allusions to many verses, passages, and ideas of Tanakh, together with rabbinic expressions with its own phraseology.

The verses relating to the prayers and blessings of this tractate are as follows:

1. Shema

The central reference used by the rabbis to support their regulations for the recitation of the *Shema* is Deut. 6:7: "And You shall teach them diligently to your children, and you shall talk of them when you sit in your house, and when you walk by the way, and when you lie down and when you rise."

The verses of the core of the *Shema* are taken from Deut. 6:4-9, Deut. 11:13-21 and Num. 15:37-41.

2.   *The verses relevant to the purity laws in M. 3:4-6:*

Deut.   23:10-14:

[Concerning a nocturnal emission:] If there is among you any man who is not clean by reason of what chances him by night, then he shall go outside the camp, he shall not come within the camp; but when evening comes on, he shall bathe himself in water and when the sun is down, he may come up within the camp.

You shall have a place outside the camp and you shall go out to it; and you shall have a stick with your weapons; and when you sit down outside, you shall dig a hole with it, and turn back and cover your excrement. Because the Lord your God walks in the midst of your camp, to save you and to give up your enemies before you, therefore your camp must be holy, that he may not see anything indecent among you, and turn away from you.

Lev.   15:16:

[Concerning a seminal emission:] And if any man had an emission of semen, he shall bathe his whole body in water, and be unclean until evening.

Lev.   15:13:

[Concerning a זב:] And when he who has a discharge is cleansed of his discharge, then he shall count for himself seven days for his cleansing, and wash his clothes; and he shall bathe his body in running water, and he shall be clean.

Lev.   15:19:

[Concerning a נדה:] When a woman has a discharge of blood which is her regular discharge from her body, she shall be in her impurity for seven days, and whoever touches her shall be unclean until the evening.

3.   *Prayer of Eighteen*

a.   The Talmud acknowledges that the Prayer was not ordained on the authority of Scripture but was instituted by the rabbis.[2]

b.   Later rabbinic authorities proposed various biblical antecedents for prayer.[3]

Some verses have been associated with the acts of Prayer:

---

[2]See B. Ber. 21a; B. Suk. 38a.

[3]See e.g. Maimonides, Laws of Prayer 1:1-8: "It is a positive commandment [of the Torah] to pray every day...."

Exod. 23:25:

> And you shall serve the Lord your God, and I will bless your bread and your water; and I will take sickness away from the midst of you.

Dan. 6:11:

> Then these men came by agreement and found Daniel making petition and supplication before his God.

c.   That prayers represent sacrifices is a concept found in Berakhot. The regulation of Temple offerings thus relates to prayer as well.

Num. 28:3-4:

> [Regarding the daily offerings:] And you shall say to them, This is the offering by fire which you shall offer to the Lord two male lambs a year old without blemish, day by day, as a continual offering. The one lamb you shall offer in the morning, and the other lamb you shall offer in the evening.

Lev. 6:2 [RSV 6:9]:

> [Regarding the limbs of the daily offering:] Command Aaron and his sons, saying, This is the law of the burnt offering. The burnt offering shall be on the hearth upon the altar all night until the morning, and the fire of the altar shall be kept burning on it.

d.   The rabbis [esp. in T. and later in B.] find elements of their conceptions of prayer in the past actions of the virtuosi of prayer in Ancient Israel:

David's prayer:

Ps. 55:17:

> Evening and morning and at noon I utter my complaint and my moan, and he will hear my voice.

Solomon's prayer in I Kings, chapter 8 [II Chron. 6], a rich source of references throughout the chapter.

e.   A verse makes allusions to the need for intention in prayer:

Ps. 10:17:

> O Lord, thou wilt hear the desire of the meek; thou wilt strengthen their heart [i.e. intention], thou wilt incline thy ear.

f.   Several references allude to postures and procedures in the prayers of some model figures in Ancient Israel.

Prayer may be silent: Hannah:

I Sam. 1:13:

> Hannah was speaking in her heart; only her lips moved, and her voice was not heard; therefore Eli took her to be a drunken woman.

Prayer may be recited while low:

Ps. 130:1:

> Out of the depths I cry to thee, O Lord!

4. Food and Meal Blessings

a. One verse makes reference to the blessings after eating:

Deut. 8:10:

> And you shall eat and you shall be satisfied and you shall bless the Lord your God.

b. There are no direct references to blessings before eating.[4]

5. Several verses are interpreted as passing allusions to other blessings.

Isa. 45:6-7:

> That men may know, from the rising of the sun and from the west, that there is none besides me; I am the Lord, and there is no other. I form light and create darkness. I make weal and create woe, I am the Lord, who do all these things.

Amos 4:13:

> For lo, he who forms the mountains, and creates the wind, and declares to man what is his thought; who makes the morning darkness, and treads on the heights of the earth—the Lord, God of hosts, is his name!

B. Berakhot in the Context of Mishnah

Our texts of M. and T. form the initial, and one of the most important, of the sixty-three tractates of M. and T. Recent scholarship on the whole corpora of M. and T. shows that they comprise self-contained tractates shaped by redactors to convey distinctive views on a variety of subjects through the discrete rules within the many chapters of the documents.[5]

When one looks at Berakhot as a component of the larger compilations of M. and of T. and examines its contents in the context of these corpora of third century Tannaitic thought one finds some of the major themes which pervade other tractates of M. present and prominent in our texts as well.

A specific Mishnaic concept in the rules of Berakhot illustrates this point. The role a person's concentration plays in the performance of the ritual of the recitation of the *Shema* (M. 2:1-2) is an important concern of the brief set of laws in chapter two of M. In a few compact lines on this subject, M. tells us

---

[4]See B. Ber. 48b for a discussion of the Scriptural basis of blessings before eating.

[5]See especially Neusner's studies cited above as well as R. Brooks, *Support for the Poor in the Mishnaic Law of Agriculture: Tractate Peah* (Chico, CA: 1983); and A.J. Peck, *The Priestly Gift in Mishnah: A Study of Tractate Terumot* (Chico, CA, 1981); P.J. Haas, *A History of the Mishnaic Law of Agriculture: Tractate Maaser Sheni*; I. Mandelbaum, *A History of the Mishnaic Law of Agriculture: Kilayim*; L. Newman, *The Sanctity of the Seventh Year: A Study of Mishnah Tractate Shebiit.*

its view of the purpose, definition, and meaning of a person's intentions. The editor of M. speaks in the familiar formulaic idiom of the document about the nature of the concentration one needs to have for the recitation of this liturgy. The tractate's few rules on the subject subtly define the nature of human intention relevant to the performance of this ritual. The laws define the character of an individual's consciousness as it pertains to the recitation of the *Shema*. Specifically, Mishnah, in the rule cited, differentiates between ordinary awareness and the state of concentration necessary for the recitation of the *Shema*. Later in the tractate, in chapter five, M. sets forth in additional regulations its view of the role of intention and concentration needed in the recitation of the Prayer of Eighteen (M. 5:1).

In the context of M. as a whole, it is not surprising to find the redactor of our tractate interested in the subject of intention. Neusner in fact has shown that the role of intention in religious actions is one of the most prominent recurring themes in M.'s tractates.[6] One might expect the texts to refer in some way to the role of one's thought or intention in the performance of religious obligations. Hence, when examining M. Berakhot's content in the light of the overall interests of M., one finds that the texts reiterate in new guises some familiar Mishnaic ideas and concepts.

Similarly, the style of Berakhot is best appreciated in the context of M. in general. When scrutinizing the literary forms and formulary patterns of the materials, one notes that our tractates draw from the limited repertoire of literary devices of Mishnaic diction found elsewhere in the corpus of texts. For the most part, the tractate, like the remainder of M., expresses its rules through a few distinctive literary patterns: patterned sentence structures, lists, groups of attributed sayings, and disputes.

By viewing M. Berakhot in this literary context, one understands better the character of some of the texts of the tractate. In particular, its most unusual stylistic unit, chapter eight, is a series of disputes between the Houses of Hillel and Shammai. This unit of Houses disputes concerning rules for the dinner stands out from the remainder of the tractate as an oddity. Its thematic concern is only indirectly linked to the main subject matter of the tractate and its literary form is noticeably different from the other materials in our compilation. This section in fact is out-of-step with the literary character of the remainder of the tractate.

However, when compared with M.'s literary choices in general throughout all of its chapters and tractates, the material in chapter eight is not at all unusual. In the larger analysis, this section represents one of the finest examples in all of M. of a coherent unit built around the Houses-dispute-form, one of M.'s most familiar formulaic structures.

---

[6]See J. Neusner, *Judaism: The Evidence of Mishnah* (Chicago: 1981), pp. 270-283.

As these examples show, the tractate is observably "Mishnaic" in both its thematic content and its formulary structure. In the context of M. as a whole, many of the issues which Berakhot takes up and many of the syntactic structures it employs are commonplace, congruent with M.'s overall style and thematic agendum. Their sometimes abrupt presence in the texts makes better sense when they are viewed as routine elements in the system of Mishnaic thought and diction.

C. Berakhot in its Social and Religious Context: Comparative data

1. Prayer in Late Antiquity

Peter Brown observes that between the second and fifth centuries the locus of divine power shifted noticeably. Late antique religious leaders developed significantly new ways of understanding and addressing God.[7] As I noted at the outset of this chapter, for Judaism, the changes in religious expression and obligation were accelerated by the forced demise of the centralized cult at the Temple in Jerusalem.

The rabbinic movement was ready to assume the mantle of religious leadership within the Jewish community made accessible to it by the changing events of the epoch. They were ready, Brown puts it, to serve as God's "exceptional human agents, who had been empowered to bring [divine power] to bear among their fellows by reason of a relationship with the supernatural that was personal to them, stable and clearly perceptible to their fellow believers."[8]

For the intellectual elite within the community of the Jews the rabbis offered a life of study, of contemplation and examination, through the philosophical system of the Mishnah and later via the Talmud. For the average folk in Jewish society they provided a world of rituals and of popular teachings. Chief among the rites they fostered were the daily and seasonal recitations of prayers and blessings, to be practiced according to the modes determined by the rabbinic expositors of religion.

2. Prayer in the Apocrypha, Pseudepigrapha and Dead Sea Scrolls[9]

The rabbis did not invent the idea of prayer. Indeed, one might easily argue that the achievements of the Psalmist in the golden age of Jewish prayer were never superceded by the rabbis, nor by other interpreters of classical liturgical expression. Jewish liturgists and theologians made various attempts to develop prayers between the era of the classical Israelite expressions of verbal praise and

---

[7]See The Making of Late Antiquity (Cambridge, MA: 1978), pp. 11-12.

[8]Brown, op. cit., p. 12.

[9]In a forthcoming study I shall more fully treat the question of the relationship between alternative forms of Jewish prayer in non-rabbinic documents and the rabbinic rules in Mishnah and Tosefta Berakhot.

petition, and the rise of the rabbinic system of liturgy. Most of these spoken expressions of worship left few traceable direct impressions on the later development of rabbinic prayer and blessings.

Let us look at some of the most prominent examples that have been described in the past. It has been argued that one may discern in the hymns and prayers of Ben Sirah, Ecclesiasticus, a prototype of a prayer similar to the rabbinic Prayer of Eighteen Blessings.[10] In Judith we find numerous short prayers some in the form of blessings.[11] In I and II Maccabees we note war prayers and thanksgiving utterances.[12] Tobit and Jubilees give us examples of prayers to be recited for safety on a journey.[13]

References to recitation of blessings at a meal may be found in the Letter of Aristeas, indicating it was a recognized pre-rabbinic Jewish practice.[14] All together Johnson collected and organized dozens of scattered references to prayer and blessing from throughout the extra-canonical literature.

While his approach is highly theological in its categories and assumptions, his work of collection presents an unambiguous picture that Jewish liturgy developed over a span of many generations. Nevertheless, the rabbinic conceptions and regulations of a system of prayer, such as we find in Mishnah, cannot be matched in scope or content in any one of the sources, nor can it be approximated by combining all the available evidence into an artificial scheme of Jewish liturgical expression.

The Dead Sea Scrolls Thanksgiving Psalms are the richest source of liturgical data from that group. These hymns need not detain us, for they provide little in the way of data parallel to our issues in tractate Berakhot.[15]

In the community rule we do note some practices for the Qumran fellowship meal which suggest some possible comparisons to our rules in chapters six through eight of Berakhot. Nevertheless, the similarities between the practices are not deep.[16]

---

[10]On this see J. Heinemann, *Prayer in the Talmud: Forms and Patterns* (N.Y.: 1977), pp. 219-221.

[11]See Norman B. Johnson, *Prayer in the Apocrypha and Pseudepigrapha* (Philadelphia: 1948), p. 8.

[12]Johnson, pp. 10-11.

[13]Johnson, pp. 12-13.

[14]Johnson, p. 15.

[15]For a full discussion of the psalms on their own terms see Svend Holm-Nielsen, *Hodayot: Psalms from Qumran* (Denmark: 1960), esp. pp. 273-359.

[16]See e.g. D. Barthelemy and J.T. Milik, *Discoveries in the Judean Desert I, Qumran Cave I* (Oxford: 1955), pp. 108ff. Also see L.H. Shiffman, "Communal Meal at Qumran," *Revue de Qumran*, Sept., 1979, 10/1, pp. 45-56. See also Heinemann, op. cit.,*passim*, and S. Talmon, "Manual of Benedictions of the Sect of the Judean Desert,"*Revue de Qumran*, volume 2, 1960, pp. 475-500.

Heinemann undertook the most ambitious attempt to categorize early rabbinic prayer in a social context, using the mode of form criticism with the goal of discovering the *sitz im leben* of each prayer and blessing in the rabbinic system.[17] A review of his work which significantly advances our understanding of many aspects of early rabbinic prayer, is beyond the scope of this introduction.

Finally, it is beyond my present range to undertake any comparison or contrast of the rules of our tractate with parallel materials in early Christianity, Gnosticism or the Hellenistic world in general. This important task I leave for another occasion.

IV. Translation and Commentary for Tractate Berakhot: The Text and its Exegesis

A. Mishnah

Mishnah Berakhot is primarily a complex tractate of formulaic Middle Hebrew religious regulations. Each coherent unit of the text, or pericope, comprises about one to five lines. The rules of M. are formulated in a highly stylized literary syntax limited to a few basic structures. These include several types of patterned declarative sentences, formal lists, and disputes between two or more authorities or schools. A major feature of the materials at hand is their attribution of laws by name to specific rabbinic authorities who lived between the first and third centuries.

In each of the following chapters I treat the materials according to the following agendum. I first offer a fresh translation of Mishnah Berakhot accompanied by an explanation of the texts. I base my translation on the critical Hebrew text of Nissan Sacks.[18] I consulted Sacks' critical apparatus throughout and also checked those manuscript facsimiles which were available to me for significant variant readings. In a few instances where a variant reading affects the meaning of a text, I include it in the body of the translation in brackets or refer to it in the commentary.

I acknowledge my debt to Danby and others who previously translated these texts. However, whereas earlier translators tended to freely paraphrase, I have striven to render the texts into English in a more literal fashion in order to better convey to the reader the literary and formal structures of the material. Because Mishnah's language is often elliptical and its syntax so stylized, I have added many phrases to the translation in brackets to provide for it greater clarity and smoothness. I also make use of different typefaces to help the reader pick out citations from the Mishnah in the Tosefta.

---

[17]Heinemann, *op. cit.*

[18]*The Mishnah with Variant Readings* (Jerusalem: 1972), vol. I, pp. 1-99.

I present the texts one chapter at a time so the reader can best follow the subject of each section of Mishnah. In the comments which accompany the texts I concentrate on explaining the meaning of the rules before us. I describe how each unit relates to its immediate context in the chapter. I also specifically ask what each tradition may tell us about the nature and historical development of early Jewish prayer. In a few cases I attend to the form of the unit in order to help explain the substance or proper context of the pericope.

B. Tosefta

Along with the texts of M. in each chapter I present the relevant passages from Tosefta, the early Tannaitic appendix to M., edited sometime between the third to fifth centuries. The individual units of this document in almost all respects resemble those of M. I find in them structures of form and syntax similar to M: formalized declarative sentences, lists, disputes, and numerous attributions to rabbinic masters. But, in its larger conception, this document is very different from M. It was redacted to serve as an appendix to M. and so must be interpreted in conjunction with Mishnah.

I find as I present T., in the context of M., that T., for the most part, explains M. and supplements it. Occasionally T. presents a short collection of its own independent materials. In the course of my presentation of the texts of M., I provide a translation of each pericope of T. at its appropriate place in the tractate.[19]

With each unit of T. I include a brief comment. My explanations for T. ask questions similar to those I pose to M.'s texts. I seek out the meaning of each rule in its context. I address special formal and substantive problems of each unit as needed. In addition I explain how each pericope in T. relates to its referent in M. Where a Toseftan unit is independent of M. I ask whether T. develops any substantial new conception of the system of early Jewish prayer.

My uppermost concern is the substantive meaning of M. and T. Berakhot. I presently turn in the following chapters to the analysis of the texts.[20]

---

[19]I base my new translation of T. on the critical edition of the Vienna Manuscript published by Saul Lieberman, *The Tosefta*, vol. I, pp. 1-40. I also consulted the English translation of A. Lukyn Williams [*Tractate Berakot (!): Mishnah and Tosefta* (New York: 1921)] and the German translation of Lohse and Schlichting [*Die Tosefta: Text/Übersetzung/Erklärung, Band I, Heft I-III*]. As I did for M., I cite in the text of the translation or in the comment to a pericope only those variants which affect the meaning of the text. I may add here that since Sack's edition of M. and Lieberman's edition of T. give full critical apparati with complete cross references to related traditions elsewhere in rabbinic literature, I do not duplicate this work in the present study.

[20]The reader who has little or no prior exposure to early rabbinic prayer may wish to refer to a standard Jewish daily prayer book to become more familiar with the full texts of the prayers and blessings to which the texts allude. A good compendium with English translations is J.H. Hertz, *The Authorized Daily Prayer Book* (New York: 1948).

Chapter One

BERAKHOT CHAPTER ONE
The Recitation of the *Shema*

The first chapter of our tractate deals with the recitation of the *Shema*, a primary prayer of rabbinic liturgy. The *Shema* is comprised of verses out of the books of Deuteronomy (6:4-9 and 11:13-21) and Numbers (15:37-41). These verses are framed before and after by rabbinic blessings, short paragraphs of prayers which express major beliefs of early rabbinic Judaism. Mishnah here does not find it necessary to tell the reader what words, verses, and paragraphs make up the *Shema*. It assumes that every adult Jew already knows them well.

Our Mishnah does not make direct reference to the historical development of the liturgy or the point of origin of this service. From Mishnah's rules one might infer that the *Shema* is timeless, that this liturgy had no history or development.

Our chapter is a short set of three rules on the proper time frame for the recitation of the *Shema* followed by two related laws. Mishnah's first and primary interest in this chapter is to delineate the time for the recitation of the *Shema* each day. When may one properly recite the *Shema* each evening and each morning?

Underlying M.'s main conception in this material is the assertion, attributed by our sources to the House of Hillel, basing the regulation to recite the *Shema* twice a day, morning and evening, on a particular understanding of the verse in scripture, "When you lie down and when you rise (Deut. 6:7)." This issue comes out clearly in the dispute between the Houses of Hillel and Shammai concerning the interpretation of this verse (M. 1:3). An account of an incident which ridicules the Shammaite view follows. In short, the first two units of the chapter (M. 1:1-2) take for granted that the Israelite recites the *Shema* every evening and morning. These initial laws serve to define the time period during which one may recite the *Shema* at the beginning and end of each day.

The chapter continues with two independent rules, M. 1:4-5, related in a general way to the point of the preceding material. M. 1:4 tells us that when one recites the *Shema* in the morning and evening, he must say the appropriate rabbinic blessings to frame the Scriptural verses of the *Shema*. The same unit adds another rule about the forms of blessings in general.

The chapter concludes at M. 1:5 with an independent tradition about the requirement to mention the exodus from Egypt in the liturgy at night. This same tradition appears elsewhere in the Passover Haggadah where it refers to the recitation of the story of the exodus on Passover Eve at the Seder. In our tractate the editors apply the rule to the regulation of the mention of the exodus in a verse of the *Shema*, Numbers 15:41. We are told that one must recite this verse at night during the recitation of the *Shema* liturgy.

This first chapter of Mishnah Berakhot then is neither a primer for the recitation of the *Shema* nor an essay on its origins and development. Nevertheless, we may deduce several facts about the development of early rabbinic prayer from this short collection of rules. First, the discussion of the manner for reciting the *Shema* is linked with the early masters, the Houses of the first century (M. 1:3). This strongly implies that the liturgy was a part of Jewish ritual during this early period. The connection of a basic issue concerning the *Shema* with first century rabbis is highly plausible and can be attested within the dynamic of the laws themselves. The next logical stages in the development of rules for the liturgy that further delineate regulations for the ritual, are associated in other sources with Yavnean masters of the following generation ca. 70-135 C.E. (M. 1:1, 1:2. 1:3G-H, 1:5).

Second, the pericope that discusses the rules for the rabbinic blessings that serve as a framework for the scriptural passages (1:4) makes no mention of any named authorities. We tend to think that it reflects concerns of the third generation, of the rabbis of Usha (ca. 135-175 C.E.). We make this inference on the supposition that the systematization of liturgical ritual grows out of the activities of the third rabbinic generation, based on our perceptions of the development of the law, spelled out in the comments to M. and T. below.

If our inferences about the historical development of the liturgy are correct, we have then in this chapter brief allusions to the development of rules for the *Shema* over three generations. The initial appearance of the *Shema* as a daily prayer occurs no later than the first century. After the destruction of the Temple additional regulations establish it as a regular daily liturgy. These rules are attributed to named authorities at Yavneh. The following generation at Usha expands the *Shema* into a more substantial rabbinic service.

With our translation of the entire chapter of M. we present the relevant Tosefta passages. The traditions in Tosefta which pertain to the first chapter of Mishnah add several comments to M. and explain some of M.'s rules. In addition, T. presents two stories relevant to M.'s interests.

Within the context of these subsidiary materials, T. introduces several important original concepts. As we shall see, M. defines the beginning of the time for the recitation of the *Shema* using the terminology of the schedule of the priests in the Temple. In contrast to this, in one tradition (1:1B), T. expresses its rule governing the time for the recitation of the evening *Shema* in terms of the timetable for eating the fellowship meal at home.

Another unit evinces a dimension in the process of the historical development of the system of rabbinic liturgy. The *Shema* and the Prayer of Eighteen, likely at first developed separately, in different eras. T. reflects a late perception which takes for granted that these two prayers are parts of one unified system of Jewish liturgy (T. 1:2C-1:3).

Another component of this segment of T. (1:6-9) discusses in one pericope two functionally distinct types of blessings. Tosefta speaks in some detail of the short blessings which serve as secondary adjuncts to other actions or rituals, such as the meal or the commandments, and the long blessings which make up the liturgy itself and thus on their own comprise the substance of independent primary rituals of prayer.

The Tosefta relevant to this chapter also supply a catalogue of specific illustrations for the general rules of M. 1:4 and of T. 1:5. In T.'s view, a short blessing is a single formula with an opening invocation and a brief conclusion. A long blessing consists of an opening invocation, several phrases to which may be added further expansions, followed by a concluding invocation and a closing phrase.

T. further supplements itself (T. 1:5) by listing those occasions where one should bow during the recitation of the prayer. In the new material at 1:9, T. goes well beyond M. and rules that in a composite liturgical setting, some long blessings do not require an opening formula because they may rely on the formula of the passage which precedes them. T. 1:8J-L adds additional independent supplements to M. A long independent unit closes out chapter one of T.

To sum up, Tosefta's material, by and large, explains and directly supplements M. In addition, T. does present here some original conceptions and thus carries forward and develops several important aspects in the development of the rules for early rabbinic prayer.

1:1

A. From what time do [people] recite the *Shema* in the evening?

B. From [after sunset, that is] the hour that the priests enter [the Temple court] to eat their heave-offering,

C. "[They may recite the *Shema* at any time thereafter up to three hours into the night, that is,] until the end of the first watch [in the Temple],"

D. the words of R. Eliezer.

E. And sages say, "[They may recite the *Shema*] until midnight."

F. Rabban Gamaliel says, "Until the break of day."

G. Once [Gamaliel's] sons came from the banquet hall.

H. And they said to him, "We have not [yet] recited the *Shema*."

I. He said to them, "If the day has not yet broken, you are obligated to recite [the *Shema*]."

J. And it is not only [in] this [case that the sages] said [that one may perform a religious obligation until daybreak]. But regarding all cases in which the sages said [that one must carry out his obligation] "until midnight," [if a person should perform] the religious obligation by daybreak [it is acceptable].

K. [For example, one may acceptably perform the obligation to] offer of the fats and entrails [of sacrifices in the Temple and to eat the paschal sacrifices] until the break of day.

L. [Another example:] All [sacrifices] which must be eaten within one day [i.e. before midnight of the day they are offered], their obligation [may legitimately be carried out and they may be eaten] until the break of day.

M. If so why did [sages] say [that these actions should be performed only] until midnight?

N. In order to keep man far from sin.

The rather complex unit which opens our tractate (1:1) is a combination of several major components. It opens with an independent pericope (A-D) consisting first of a question and answer (A-B) about the time from which one may recite the *Shema* in the evening. The question is straightforward. The roundabout answer chooses to define the time for recitation of liturgy in terminology of the Temple schedule. One recites the *Shema* after the time that priests who were unclean by day may enter to eat sancta at night, i.e. after nightfall. This indirect mode of response continues at C with the additional rule for defining the *end* of the time for reciting the *Shema*. One may recite until the conclusion of the first watch of the four watches in the Temple. D attributes the preceding to Eliezer.

The unit A-D in one way is not totally consistent because C answers more than A asks. But, on the other hand, B and C closely relate to one another. Both draw on Temple imagery for defining the limits of the time period for reciting the *Shema*. D apparently attributes at least C, and probably B, to Eliezer. In any event, the tradition adumbrates an important idea in the rabbinic explanation and justification of the liturgical system. That is, prayer first extends, then replaces, the Temple service.

E-F appends two contrary rulings to the latter part of the preceding (C-D). Sages and Gamaliel both dispute Eliezer's ruling regarding the latest time to recite the *Shema*. The views, here presented in direct terms, not through analogy to the routine of the Temple cult, extend the allowable time period for reciting the *Shema* to midnight or to dawn respectively. Gamaliel's opinion is defended on two grounds. Mishnah first bolsters the view on the basis of a precedent (G-I) (which indeed may have been the earlier source in rabbinic tradition which generated the lemma giving his view). Then Mishnah continues with support for Gamaliel on the strength of analogies from other rules (J-L). Not surprisingly, M. compares this law with rules elsewhere for some Temple sacrifices which *should be* eaten or offered by midnight but *may be* consumed or sacrificed until the dawn. So too the *Shema* may be recited until dawn.

The overall unit concludes with an explanation of sages' position. Apparently Gamaliel is right, the obligation to recite persists until dawn. But sages provide a safer alternative. One must finish the ritual and recite by midnight to guard oneself from inadvertently transgressing the law.

This pericope gives us a sense of the potential complexity of M.'s rules. It combines a composite dispute (A-F) with a precedent (G-I), legal analogy (J-L), and a compromise (M-N). This first pericope is one of the most complicated of M.'s units in our tractate.

T. 1:1

A. *From what time do [people] recite the Shema in the evening?*

B. "[They may recite the *Shema*] from the hour that people are accustomed to enter [their houses] to eat their bread on Sabbath eve," the words of R. Meir.

C. And sages say, *"From [after sunset, that is] the hour that the priests enter [the Temple court] to eat their heave-offering."*

D. [Regarding the recitation of the *Shema*, when does night begin?] We may find an indication for [the time night begins is the verse] "Until the stars came out [Neh. 4:15=RSV 4:21].

E. Even though there is no proof [in Scripture that night begins when the stars come out], there is an allusion [in the verse,] "So we labored at the work and half of them held the spears from the break of dawn until the stars came out [Neh. 4:21]." [The passage continues, "Let every man and his servant pass the night within Jerusalem, that they may be a guard for us by night and may labor by day [Neh. 4:22]." They labored until night, i.e. when the stars came out. These verses imply that it is night when the stars come out.]

F. R. Simeon says, "Sometimes one recites the *Shema* [twice in one night,] once before the dawn and once after the dawn,

G. and we find that he fulfills his obligation for the [recitations of the *Shema*] of the day and of the night."

H. Rabbi says, "There are four watches [אשמורות] in the day and four watches in the night."

I. The עונה is one twenty-fourth of an hour. The עת is one twenty-fourth of a עונה. The רגע is one twenty-fourth of an עת.

J. R. Nathan says, "There are three watches in the night.

K. "As it says, 'At the beginning of the middle watch' [Judges 7:19].

L. "There can be no middle [watch] unless there is [a watch] before it and after it."

T. 1:1 is in four parts. First A-D is an alternative to M. 1:1A-B. T. gives us a dispute between the Ushan master Meir and the anonymous sages. (T. does not assign M.'s B to Eliezer.) There is no real substance to this dispute because both opinions refer to the same time of day, sunset, but express it in different ways. As we noted in explaining M. above, sages draw their analogy from the Temple time schedule. Meir connects the rule for recitation of the *Shema* with the practice for the more familiar rabbinic Sabbath fellowship meal, rather than the less familiar cultic Temple nomenclature of past generations.

T.'s second part (E-F) is an independent supplement to M. It defines the earliest time for the evening *Shema* in terms of objective astronomical observation of stars. When it is dark enough to see stars one may recite (and we presume likewise one may eat heave-offering or the Sabbath meal). The unit provides a scriptural basis for the definition.

In the third segment of T., Simeon, an Ushan, indirectly elaborates on the opinion of the Yavnean master, Gamaliel, concerning the latest hour for reciting the evening *Shema* (M. 1:1F). Simeon carries the rule to its logical but curious, conclusion. One may recite the *Shema* twice in immediate succession, right before and after daybreak and get credit for saying both the evening and morning *Shema*. This Ushan observation builds on Gamaliel's rule, thus better attesting the latter attribution to Yavneh. But at the same time it implicitly calls the sagacity of the law into question and seems to support either Eliezer or sages' view (M. 1:1 C-E).

The last part of this T. (H-L) is an independent unit which serves as a supplement to Eliezer's ruling that one may recite the *Shema* until the end of the first watch (1:1C). T. gives a dispute between two later masters, Rabbi and Nathan, with scriptural proof text for the latter position. The interjection (J) is an independent explanation, not directly related to our concerns.

For the purposes of reconstructing the conceptual-historical development of the liturgy, Meir's lemma (B-C) is the main item of interest in this unit. It shows that no later than in Ushan times, one master chose to define regulations for liturgy by drawing analogy out of the practice of the fellowship meal, rather than from the schedule of the long-gone Temple.

1:2

    A. From what time do they recite the *Shema* in the morning?

    B. From [the time that] one can distinguish between blue and white.

    C. R. Eliezer said, "Between blue and green."

    D. [And one completes the recitation] before sunrise.

    E. R. Joshua says. "[One may recite] until the third hour."

    F. "For it is the practice of royalty to rise at the third hour."

    G. One who recites after this time has not lost [the purpose of the act for he is] like one who recites [passages] from the Torah.

M.'s next concern, the time for reciting the morning *Shema,* is an unresolved issue at Yavneh. The question here (A) parallels the corresponding query of M. 1:1 for the evening *Shema*. Line A asks by what criterion we determine whether it is light enough to recite the *Shema* in the morning? Both the anonymous view and Eliezer (B-C) respond. Eliezer disputes B. He demands that it be lighter before one may recite.

The second issue of the pericope (until when one may recite?) is clearly separated from the first. According to D, one may recite until sunrise. Joshua disagrees. He permits recitation at a much later time. His rationale (F) reflects the Hillelite view of 1:3F, that one recites at the time people arise, which, for royalty, may be late in the morning.

The ritual of the *Shema* then, as defined by M. 1:1-2, is the recitation of the appropriate verses twice each day in the proper time frames. One who recites the verses at other times does not fulfill his obligation to recite the *Shema*. But, as G observes, even reciting late has some salvageable value. It is at least as worthwhile as recitation of verses from the Torah, an act of study, which always bears merit.

In the last remark (G), M. conveys the primary rabbinic mechanism for transforming scriptural passages into liturgy. In order for these verses from Torah to become "prayer" they first must be set into a specific ritual and performed within a specified frame of time. Outside the frame of the ritual, the verses are not liturgical. They remain, at most, Torah passages.

T. 1:2

A. *From what time do they recite the Shema in the morning?*

B. Others say, "[Before one recites the *Shema* it should be daylight enough] so that one may be four cubits from his fellow and recognize him."

C. [Concerning the requirement to recite the *Shema* in the morning they said,] "Its obligation is [best fulfilled] at sunrise so that one may adjoin [the blessing following the *Shema* called] 'Redemption' to the Prayer [of Eighteen blessings] and it turns out that [thereby] he recites the Prayer in the daytime."

D. Said R. Judah, "Once I was walking on the road behind R. Eleazar b. Azariah and behind R. Aqiba. And the time came [at sunrise] for the recitation of the *Shema* [and they did not recite].

E. "And I thought that they perhaps had neglected to recite the *Shema* [that morning].

F. "Rather [they did not have time to recite] because they were preoccupied with [urgent] communal needs.

G. "I recited [the *Shema*] and studied and afterwards they began."

H. "And the sun [had risen earlier and] was already visible across the mountaintops."

T. first supplements M. providing a third opinion to the two disputing views of M. 1:2 B-C. This alternative (B) appears to require that one wait until it is a bit later in the morning before one recites.

C explains why one should complete the recitation by sunrise (M.1:1D). This important lemma suggests that one may then adjoin the *Shema* to the Prayer of Eighteen and recite both at the best proper times. Most of our other sources elsewhere in the tractate suggest that these two liturgies developed separately. While the *Shema* may have its roots back in the early first century (cf. M. 1:3), mention of the Prayer of Eighteen appears at the earliest in Yavnean materials (cf. M. 4:3). After originating and developing independently, it is logical to assume that the liturgies converged in the systematization of rabbinic prayer. The brief remark at C suggests that one stage in such a process did occur. The rule is that one must adjoin the two liturgies together at the best possible time, at daybreak, probably stems from the generation of the Ushan masters, the most thorough early systematizers of rabbinic law and ritual.

The story D-H supplements M. 1:2 D-G. Although it indicates that the two Yavneans recited after sunrise, the present version does not necessarily support Joshua's view that one may recite until the third hour. The gloss (F) declares that communal needs delayed the rabbis. Under ordinary circumstances, we assume, they should have recited before sunrise in accord with the anonymous view of M. 1:2D.

This unit's primary importance for recovering the history of early rabbinic prayer is its implication of the late second century convergence of separate liturgies into an integrated system of prayer, as explained above.

1:3

A. The House of Shammai says, "In the evening everyone should recline and recite [the *Shema*], and in the morning they should stand.

B. "As it says, 'When you lie down and when you rise' [Deut. 6:7]."

C. And the House of Hillel says, "Everyone recites according to his own manner."

D. "As it says, 'And you walk by the way' [ibid]."

E. If so why does [the verse] say, "When you lie down and when you rise up?"

F. [It means recite the *Shema*] at the hour that people lie down [at night] and at the hour that people rise up [in the morning].

G. Said. R. Tarfon, "I was coming by the road and I reclined to recite the *Shema* in accordance with the words of the House of Shammai. And I placed myself in danger of [attack by] bandits."

H. They said to him, "Fittingly, you have only yourself to blame [for what might have befallen you]. For you violated the words of the House of Hillel."

The Houses dispute the meaning of the verse, "When you lie down and when you rise." The Shammaites interpret that this refers to one's posture for reciting—reclining in the evening, standing in the morning. The Hillelites at C-D reject this. The story at G-H derides the Shammaite view. Tarfon endangered himself by adhering to the Shammaite practice.

The Hillelite alternate exegesis of the verse, presented at E-F, serves to support the basic premise of this first chapter of M. It provides Scriptural support for the notion that there are specific time periods for the recitation of the morning and evening *Shema*.

T. 1:3

A. Bridegrooms and all those engaged in [the performance of] commandments are exempt from [the obligation of] reciting the *Shema* and the Prayer.

B. As Scripture states, "When you sit in your house," [this] excludes those who are [out] engaged in fulfilling commandments [from the obligation to recite the *Shema*]. And "When you walk by the way," [this] excludes the bridegroom [because he is involved in the obligations of marriage].

T. 1:3 says that the verse cited in M. 1:3 also serves as the basis for excluding the bridegroom and one who is performing other commandments from the obligation to recite the *Shema* (cf. M. 2:5, 2:8) and the prayer. One might read this latter exclusion as a support to justify the gloss to the story in the preceding, T. 1:2F, that explained why Aqiba and Eleazar b. Azariah recited after the appointed time in the morning.

Note that T. here presents a single rule for two components of the liturgy, both the *Shema* and Prayer.

T. 1:4

A. *M'sh:* Once R. Eleazar b. Azariah and R. Ishmael were staying in one place. And R. Ishmael was reclining and R. Eleazar b. Azariah was standing upright. When the time came for the recitation of the *Shema* [in the evening (Lieberman)], R. Ishmael sat up and R. Eleazar b. Azariah reclined.

B. Said to him R. Ishmael, "What is [the meaning of your action], Eleazar?"

C. Said [R. Eleazar b. Azariah] to him [R. Ishmael], "Ishmael my brother [I will give you an analogy to explain my action]. If they say to an individual, 'Why do you grow your beard long?' And he says, 'It is a protest against the destroyers [who cut their beards. I did this to show my disagreement with those who hold a different custom. But there is no other reason for it].'"

D. [Likewise,] "I who was standing, reclined [to recite to show that I do not hold the Hillelite view]. And you, who were reclining, arose [showing that you do not follow the Shammaites]."

E. He [Ishmael] said to him, "[I disagree. There is a positive indication in our actions. Eleazar,] you reclined in accordance with the words of the House of Shammai [who said to recite while reclining]. And I arose in accordance with the words of the House of Hillel [who said one may recite in any position]."

F. An alternate explanation: "[I, Ishmael, agree with how you put it, Eleazar. I arose] so that the students should not observe me and establish the law in accordance with the words of the House of Shammai."

Although the exact meaning of the term "destroyers" in D is not known, its implication is clear. Eleazar says that Ishmael's action is a protest against Eleazar's action which accorded with the Shammaite view that one must recline for the recitation of the evening *Shema* (M. 1:3A). The story incidentally further indicates that some basic regulations for reciting the *Shema* were open issues even in the middle of the second century, the period of rabbinic activity at Yavneh.

I give for F the version of the first printed edition. There are several versions of this story elsewhere with variants which significantly alter its meaning. For a discussion see my *Eleazar*, pp. 16-21.

1:4

A. In the morning one recites two blessings before [the *Shema*] and one after it.

B. And in the evening two before it and two after it.

C. Whether a long or a short [blessing, the rule is the same].

D. Where they said to lengthen [the formula of a blessing by both beginning and ending with the formula "Blessed art Thou"] one is not permitted to shorten it [by omitting it].

E. [Where they said] to shorten [by only beginning with "Blessed art Thou," one is not permitted to lengthen it by also closing with "Blessed art Thou"].

F. [Where they said] to seal [a blessing with the formula "Blessed art Thou" at the end], one is not permitted not to seal.

G. [Where they said] not to seal, one is not permitted to seal [by adding to it].

A rabbinic liturgical framework accompanies the scriptural verses of the liturgy of the *Shema.* M. tells us that two blessings (i.e. two short paragraphs of rabbinic liturgy concluding with blessings) precede and one follows in the morning recitation. Two precede and two follow in the evening liturgy.

Now, let us review the components of the rabbinic liturgy presented by M. in this chapter. M. specified two components of the ritual which define the *Shema:* the time-frame for its recitation and the rabbinic framework of blessings in which one recites the scriptural passages.

The latter, the framework of blessings, appears to be a later component of the ritual, appended at Usha in a period of the reformulation of the liturgy. In addition we propose that the accompanying independent anonymous rules at C-G which regulate the forms of blessings also stem from the Ushan period.

C-G refers to three liturgical forms. First, the short blessing is of the form, "Blessed art Thou O Lord our God" + a short phrase. Second, the long blessing which is not sealed is in the pattern, "Blessed art Thou..." + several phrases, sentences, or a paragraph. Third, the long blessing which is sealed makes use of the construct, "Blessed art Thou..." + phrases, sentences or a paragraph, + "Blessed art Thou..." + a short phrase which usually recapitulates a main theme of the preceding liturgy. Clearly C-G is an important unit, but only generally related to the present context. Its rules certainly should appear in our tractate. Apparently, for lack of a better place, M.'s editors inserted them here.

T. 1:5

A. [With regard to the length of the blessings before the evening recitation of the *Shema*, M. Ber. 1:4], why did they say [one long and] one short?

B. Where they prescribed a long blessing, one is not permitted to recite a short blessing;

[where they prescribed] a short blessing, one is not permitted to recite a long blessing.

C. [Where they prescribed] to conclude [lit., "seal"] [a blessing with the benedictory formula, "Blessed art Thou, O Lord..."], one is not permitted not to conclude it [thus];

[where they prescribed] not to conclude [a blessing in this way] one is not permitted [thus] to conclude [it] [B-C = M. Ber. 1:4D-E].

D. [Where they prescribed] to bow, one is not permitted not to bow;

[where they prescribed] not to bow, one is not permitted to bow.

E. [Where they prescribed] to begin [a blessing] with [the words,] "Blessed [art Thou, O Lord our God..."; viz., the stereotype rabbinic benedictory formula], one is not permitted not to begin with "Blessed [art Thou...]";

[where they prescribed] not to begin with "Blessed [art Thou...]," one is not permitted to begin with "Blessed [art Thou...]."

T. 1:6

A. These are the blessings [whose formulae] they may shorten: [those recited over] the produce [one eats], over the [performance of individual] Commandments, the blessing of the invitation [to recite the other blessings after the meal], and the last meal-blessing after the meal.

B. These are the blessings [whose formulae] they may lengthen: those blessings [in the Prayer recited on] public fast days, and those blessings [in the Prayer recited on] the New Year, and those blessings [in the Prayer recited on] the Day of Atonement.

C. From a man's [style of reciting] blessings one can tell whether he is a boor or a disciple of the sages.

T. 1:7

D. These are the blessings which one does not conclude [with a benedictory formula]:

he who recites a blessing [1] upon [eating] produce and [2] upon the [performance of the] commandments, [3] and the invitation [to grace], [4] and the final blessing of the grace after meals.

E. R. Yose the Galilean used to conclude [with a benedictory formula] the final blessing of the grace after meals and recite it at length.

T. 1:8

F. These are the blessings for which they bow [when they recite them]: For the first [paragraph of the Prayer of Eighteen at the] beginning and end [of the paragraph, for the eighteenth blessing,] "We give thanks," [at the] beginning and end.

G. One who bows for each and every blessing [of the Prayer of Eighteen,] they instruct him not to bow [so that he should not appear arrogant].

T. 1:9

H. These are the blessings which begin with [the formula] "Blessed [art Thou...]."

All the blessings begin with "Blessed," (V. omits the preceding phrase) except, the blessings which adjoin the recitation of *Shema* and any blessing which adjoins another blessing [in serial fashion].

I. They need not begin these with [the formula] "Blessed" [because the formula from the first blessing suffices],

J. and one does not respond together with the [leader of the congregation who] recites the blessings [simultaneously, but must answer responsively to his recitation (Lieberman)].

K. R. Judah would respond together with the prayer-leader [in the Qedusha, or sanctificatory sequence], "Holy, holy, holy is the Lord of Hosts; the whole earth is full of his glory [Isa. 6:3]," and "Blessed be the glory of the Lord [Ezek. 3:12]."

L. All these [responses] R. Judah would recite together with the prayer-leader.

To supplement M. 1:4, T. 1:6 A-B provides lists of blessings which must be short or which one may lengthen. 1:7D lists those same blessings again as examples of those which one does not recite the closing formula. Yose glosses at E. 1:8 F-G deals with bowing while reciting blessings. It further expands upon T. 1:5 C-D above. 1:9 H-I gives additional regulation for the form of a blessing. One may omit the opening formula from one blessing which is adjacent to another. J-L discusses procedures for reciting several additional verses in the liturgy after the scriptural passages of the *Shema*. J says they do not recite the blessings after the *Shema* simultaneously with the leader. Judah, according to K-L, recited these two verses along with the leader. Apparently that practice should be emulated.

T. 1:6C interjects an interesting observation into this unit. One can tell about a man by listening to his blessings. One who recites them incorrectly is a boor. One who knows the system of blessings is a disciple of the sages.

Based on this unit we may draw several preliminary conclusions concerning the development of the liturgy. First, as I said above, the general systematization of prayers and blessings is an Ushan undertaking. As we see T. 1:9 K-L refers to Judah's practice during the recitation of the blessings following the *Shema*, which I take as an indication of the Ushan provenance of this framework for the *Shema*.

Second, in reference to another part of the liturgy, T. 1:7E links a Yavnean, Yose the Galilean, with the blessings for the meal, suggesting that as the formative era for the development of the meal blessings. The issues of the origin and early formation of these blessings will be discussed further in the comments to M. 6:8.

1:5

A. They mention the exodus from Egypt at night.

B. Said R. Eleazar b. Azariah to them, "I am like a seventy-year-old and was not worthy [of understanding why] the exodus from Egypt [in the third paragraph of the *Shema*] is said [in the recitation] at night until Ben Zoma expounded it."

C. As it says, "So that all the days of your life you may remember the day when you came out of the land of Egypt" [Deut. 16:3].

D. "The days of your life" [implies only] the days. "All the days of your life" [includes] the nights.

E. And sages say, "The days of your life' [includes only your life in] this world. 'All the days of your life' also encompasses the messianic age."

M. 1:5A is a second independent appendage to the core concerns of this chapter. Up to this point we dealt with the form, not the content, of the recitation of the *Shema*. Most commentaries say this present lemma refers to the last verse of the third scriptural paragraph (Num. 15:41) which mentions the exodus. Lieberman, citing GRA and others in accord with references in T. 2:1, says this is an allusion to the mention of the exodus in the rabbinic blessings which follow the *Shema*.

Eleazar's view (B-D) supports the opening lemma (A). Sages dispute it (E). As we indicated, the whole unit B-E can be read independent of the present context. The statement appears for instance in the Passover Haggadah to justify reciting the story of the exodus on Passover eve.

Though this unit is basically peripheral to the rest of the chapter which precedes it, we may infer from M. 1:5 that the fixing of the exact scriptural passages comprising the recitation of the *Shema* was still an open issue at Yavneh.

T. 1:10

A. *They mention the exodus from Egypt at night.*

B. *Said R. Eleazar b. Azariah to them, "I am like a seventy-year-old and was not worthy [of understanding why] the exodus from Egypt [in the third paragraph of the Shema] is said [in the recitation] at night until Ben Zoma expounded it."*

C. *As it says, "So that all the days of your life you may remember the day when you came out of the land of Egypt"* [Deut. 16:3]

D. *"The days of your life" [implies only] the days. "All the days of your life" [includes] the nights.*

E. *And sages say, "The days of your life' [includes only your life in] this world. 'All the days of your life' also encompasses the messianic age"* [M. Ber. 1:5].

F. Said to them Ben Zoma, "But does one mention the exodus from Egypt in the messianic age?

G. "For has it not already been said, Therefore, behold, the days are coming, says the Lord, when men shall no longer say 'As the Lord lives who brought up the people of Israel out of the land of Egypt,' but, 'As the Lord lives who brought up and led the descendants of the house of Israel out of the north country [and out of all the countries where he had driven them]' [Jer. 23:7-8]?"

H. They said to him, "It is not that [mention of] the exodus from Egypt will be removed from its place [in the liturgy], but that the exodus from Egypt will be [mentioned] in addition to [the restoration of God's] Sovereignty. Sovereignty [will be] primary and the exodus from Egypt [will be] secondary" [cf. T. Ber. 2:1].

I. Similarly, No longer shall your name be called Jacob, but Israel shall be your name [Gen. 35:10]. It is not that the name Jacob will be taken from him but that [he shall be called] Jacob in addition to Israel. Israel will be [his] primary [name] and Jacob [his] secondary [name].

T. 1:11

J. Similarly, "Remember not the former things, nor consider the things of old" [Isa. 43:18]. "Remember not the former things"–these are [God's mighty acts in saving Israel] from the [various] kingdoms; "nor consider things of old"–these are [God's mighty acts in saving Israel] from Egypt.

K. "Behold, I am doing a new thing; now it springs forth" [Isa. 43:19]–this refers to the war of Gog and Magog [at the end of time].

L. They drew a parable, to what may the matter be compared? To one who was walking in the way and a wolf attacked him, but he was saved from it. He would continually relate the incident of the wolf. Later a lion attacked him, but he was saved from it. He forgot the incident of the wolf and would relate the incident of the lion. Later still a serpent attacked him, but he was saved from it. He forgot the other two incidents and would continually relate the incident of the serpent.

M. So, too are Israel: the recent travails make them forget about the earlier ones.

T. 1:12

N. Similarly, "No longer shall your name be Abram, but your name shall be Abraham" [Gen. 17:5]. At first you were the father of Aram [the Arameans]. Now you are the father of the entire world, as Scripture states, "For I have made you the father of a multitude of nations" [ibid].

T. 1:13

O. Similarly, "As for Sarai your wife, you shall not call her name Sarai, but Sarah shall be her name" [Gen. 17:15]. At first she was the ruler of her people. Now she rules over all the world. As it says, "But Sarah shall be her name" [srh = ruler].

T. 1:14

P. Even though he [God] again called Abraham Abram [after changing the name], it was not by way of blame but rather in praise. [Even though God again called] Joshua Hosea, it was not by way of blame but rather in praise.

Q. He was called Abram before [God] spoke with him and Abraham after [God] spoke with him. He was called Hosea before he was appointed to high position and Joshua after he was appointed to high position.

R. "Moses Moses," "Abraham Abraham," "Jacob Jacob," "Samuel Samuel" [i.e., God's repetition of their names in addressing these men in various scriptural verses]—all these [repetitions] are expressions of endearment, expressions of encouragement, equally applicable before [God] spoke with them and after he spoke with them, before they were appointed to high position and after they were appointed to high position.

T. 1:15

S. Similarly, "His abode has been established in Salem, his dwelling place in Zion" [Ps. 76:3 [=RSV 76:2]]. Why does Scripture revert to using its [Jerusalem's] former name? Because it says, "This city has aroused my anger and my wrath" [Jeremiah 32:31]. One might [erroneously] assume [from this verse] that even now it is regarded [by God] with anger and wrath. [Therefore] Scripture states [to the contrary], "At the mount which God desired for His abode [Ps. 68:17 [=RSV 68:16]]. Behold, it is [regarded by God] with loving desire and craving. This teaches that its destruction effected atonement for it.

T. And from what [scriptural verse] do we learn that the Divine Presence does not return to its [Zion's] midst until it becomes [again] a [desolate] mountain [that is, until the Temple is destroyed and the site is reduced again to the status of a desolate mountain]? As Scripture states, "His abode has been established in Salem." We find that when it [the Temple Mount] was [yet] Salem, it was called a mountain. Thus, the Divine Presence does not return to it until it becomes [again] a [desolate] mountain [viz., God's abode was established in Zion even before the Temple was built, while the Mount was still Salem, and so will it be again].

U. And Scripture states, "So Abraham called the name of that place The Lord will provide;" as it is said to this day, "On the Mount of the Lord it shall be provided" [Gen. 22:14].

V. And Scripture states, "Remember, O Lord, against the Edomites the day of Jerusalem. When? When its foundations will have been uprooted, How they said, 'Raze it, raze it! Down to its foundations!'" [Ps. 137:7].

T. 1:10 A-E cites M. 1:5 A-E. T. then proceeds to develop its own concern, namely, what changes will be made to the liturgy in the messianic age? T. says the liturgy will be emended at that time to include both the mentions of the redemption from Egypt and the messianic kingship (F-I). Ultimately, in the time of Gog and Magog at the end of days (T. 1:11-13), both references will be superseded. The remaining units (1:14-15) focus on the significance of the change by God of a name of a person or place, a matter related in a more tangential way to the preceding interests of Tosefta.

T. 2:1

A. One who recites the *Shema* [in the morning] must mention the exodus from Egypt in [the blessing which follows the *Shema* and begins with the words] "True and upright."

B. Rabbi says, "One must mention [God's] kingship in [that paragraph]."

C. Others say, "One must mention the [miracles of the] the smiting of the first-born and the splitting of the sea."

T. complements M. 1:5. It rules that the blessings which follow the *Shema* in the morning must contain a special reference to the exodus. Rabbi adds that it must also mention kingship. C cites a view which requires two other references in the same liturgy.

If the attribution of B to Rabbi is accepted, we may assume that the content of the rabbinic liturgical framework of the *Shema* apparently was still somewhat of an open issue even in post-Ushan times, a possible indication that its origin may go back only to the preceding generation, to Usha.

Chapter Two

Further Laws for the Recitation of the Shema

This chapter defines several central components of the rabbinic ritual of the recitation of the *Shema*. Mishnah tells us first that one must concentrate during his recitation in order to properly fulfill his commanded obligation (2:1A). Next our chapter defines as best it can, the nature of the concentration which must accompany the recitation. Mishnah has no way to describe directly the internal state of mind that one must have during the ritual. So instead, it discusses the way one must alter his relationship to external distractions in order to achieve the correct state of mind for reciting the *Shema*. Mishnah expresses this concept through a dispute over the propriety of exchanging greetings during the recitation of the *Shema*.

M. says one must filter out of one's thoughts some of the ordinary distractions of the external world, such as the presence of other persons. Even though normally one would greet certain parties, while engaged in the recitation of the *Shema,* one must refrain from engaging in some kinds of social contact (2:1D-G). That is how Mishnah articulates its idea of the required state of consciousness for the ritual.

Two Ushan masters disagree in M. over the extent to which one must refrain from exchanging a greeting. But they agree in principle that during one's recitation of the *Shema* one must refrain from some aspect of ordinary social interaction. In this indirect way, Mishnah defines an important dimension of the nature of concentration which must accompany the *Shema*.

Ushan masters dispute, as we have seen, the finer points of the nature of the intention which one must have for the *Shema*. An earlier authority, the Yavnean rabbi, Joshua B. Qorha, then provides, as an independent addition to the preceding, a basic explanation for the order of the paragraphs of the *Shema* (2:2H-K). The chapter next turns briefly (2:3) to rules for the actual recitation of the words of the *Shema*. They must be articulated, clearly and in order, without error. Our unit makes it clear that two components, proper mental concentration and accurate verbal recitation, together comprise two main ingredients of the ritual.

At 2:4 the chapter returns to its initial theme, and further defines the kind of concentration one needs for recitation of the *Shema*. The next few rulings deal a bit more indirectly with this subject. M. refers to two kinds of distractions which are significant enough to disrupt one's concentration, fear of heights and the emotions of the newlywed (2:4-5 and 2:8). The unit then digresses briefly to add two rulings concerning Gamaliel at 2:6-7 to complete a set of three traditions about this master begun at 2:5.

The Yavneans in this chapter discuss some basic notions of the *Shema* such as the order of the scriptural passages and the obligation of the bridegroom to recite.   Ushans deal with finer distinctions concerning the nature of the concentration which accompanies the *Shema* and the regulations for the recitation itself. As pointed out, there is at best a subtle distinction between the conflicting Ushan opinions in the dispute over these rules. All in all, from this chapter we can infer little about the linear historical development of the *Shema*.

Nonetheless, the present chapter adds significantly to our understanding of how the rabbis defined some key aspects of the ritual of the recitation of the *Shema*. Chapter one, we recall, defined the timeframe and liturgical-frame for the recitation of the verses of the *Shema*. Our present material goes on to define the frame of mind and the necessary accuracy in enunciation that one must have in his recitation, important aspects of the essential definition of the *Shema* ritual.

Overall the corresponding passages in T. supplement M.'s topics with related rules. What is entirely new in T. is a special regulation for workers as a class (T. 2:9). They may recite the prayers and blessings but may not lead the congregation in public recitation.

2:1

A. One who was reciting from the Torah [at Deut. 6:4] and the time came for the recitation of the *Shema*,

B. If he had intention [to do so] he fulfilled his obligation [to recite the *Shema*].

C. And if he did not [have intention to do so], he did not fulfill his obligation.

D. "At the breaks [between the paragraphs of the *Shema*] one may extend a greeting [to his fellow] out of respect, and respond [to a greeting extended to him].

E. "And in the middle [of reciting a paragraph] one may extend a greeting out of fear and respond," the words of R. Meir.

F. R. Judah says, "In the middle [of a paragraph] one may extend a greeting out of fear and respond out of respect.

G. "At the breaks [between the paragraphs] one may extend a greeting out of respect and respond to the greeting of any man."

This chapter focuses first on rules related to the state of mind necessary for the *Shema*. At 2:1A M. presents a case of a person who recites the words of the *Shema* at the time for the recitation, but who says them ostensibly for another purpose, for the recitation of Scripture, not of liturgy. C says that recitation alone is not enough to fulfill the obligation to recite the *Shema*. To discharge one's obligation, to perform the ritual of reciting the *Shema,* a person must actively intend to fulfill his obligation. So M. here rules that to properly recite the *Shema* one must speak the prescribed text while maintaining a special state of concentration.

It is difficult to directly define in a few words the nature of the concentration needed to properly perform this ritual. Instead M. specifies how, during the recitation, one must alter his relationship to the external distractions of the world around him, so that he may properly direct his internal consciousness. M. sets this forth in its stylized idiom through the dispute at D-G.

Judah and Meir disagree concerning the propriety of extending or returning a greeting while reciting the *Shema*. According to both rabbis one may vary his level of concentration during one's recitation. Meir (D-E) says that between paragraphs one may relax his concentration and extend a normal greeting out of respect as in ordinary discourse. But while in the midst of reciting a paragraph, one may not lapse into an ordinary state of mind to extend or respond to a greeting except if he fears the consequences of ignoring some important person close by.

Judah is more lenient. While reciting a paragraph one may certainly extend a greeting to a person of authority whom he fears and one may respond even to a person deserving respect. Between sections of the *Shema,* one may carry on nearly the ordinary exchange of greetings. He may greet a person he respects and answer the greeting of any ordinary person.

Both rabbis agree that one's concentration on the recitation of the *Shema* establishes a state of mind which requires a person to modify his relation to the other people nearby. Their dispute concerns the intensity of this change in ordinary social interaction necessary during the heightened consciousness of the recitation of the *Shema.*

2:2

A. These are the breaks [in the *Shema*]:

B. Between the first blessing and the second [of those which precede the scriptural passages of the *Shema*].

C. Between the second blessing and [the second paragraph which begins] "Hear O Israel" [Deut. 6:4-9].

D. Between [the two sections which begin] "Hear O Israel" and "And it shall come to pass if you shall hearken [Deut. 11:13-21]."

E. Between [the two sections beginning] "And it shall come to pass" and "And God said to Moses [Num. 15:37-41]."

F. Between [the two sections] "And God said" and "True and upright" [the blessing which follows the scriptural passages].

G. R. Judah said, "Between [the two sections] 'And God said' and 'True and upright' one may not interrupt."

H. Said R. Joshua b. Qorha, "Why does [the recitation of] 'Hear O Israel' precede [the recitation of] 'And it shall come to pass'?

I. "So that one should first accept upon himself the yoke of the kingdom of heaven [by reciting the first paragraph] and afterwards [accept] the yoke of the commandments [by reciting the second paragraph]."

J. "[Why does the recitation of] 'And it shall come to pass' [precede the recitation of] 'And God said'?

K. "For 'And it shall come to pass' is recited both by day and night. 'And God said' is recited only by day." [The principle is that a more frequent requirement takes precedence over a less frequent requirement.]

M. continues with three traditions that develop the preceding points. First at A-F, M. defines "the breaks" mentioned earlier at 2:1 A-E. Judah, at G, takes exception to the last element of that definition. Joshua ben Qorha then provides, at H-K, a brief justification for the order of the paragraphs, an issue tangential to the present context. The comment at K that one says the third paragraph (Num. 15:37-41) only in the morning *Shema* implies that at Yavneh some recited a shortened evening *Shema*, a practice later changed. Added to the preceding basic materials in M. attributed to Yavneans regarding the *Shema*, this serves as another indication that in the period after the destruction of the Temple the rabbis sought to define and establish a regular daily liturgical order which then took systematic shape in the subsequent generation at Usha.

T. 2:2

A. One who recites the *Shema* must concentrate.

B. R. Ahai says in the name of R. Judah, "If one had intention [to fulfill his obligation] during his recitation of the first paragraph, even though he did not have intention during his recitation of the second paragraph, he fulfilled his obligation."

T. says directly what M. takes for granted–that one must have specific intention when reciting the *Shema* (A). B recognizes the potential practical limitation of a person's power of concentration.

2:3

A. One who recites the *Shema* but does not articulate it [out loud] fulfills his obligation.

B. R. Yose says, "He did not fulfill his obligation."

C. If he recited but was not careful about [pronunciation of] the letters [of each word]–

D. R. Yose says, "He fulfilled his obligation."

E. R. Judah says, "He did not fulfill his obligation."

F. One who recites it backwards [i.e. recites the verses or paragraphs out of order] does not fulfill his obligation.

G. One who recited and erred–he must return to the place where he erred [and repeat his recitation].

M. appropriately turns from its discussion of the state of mind needed for the *Shema* to the regulations for the verbal recitation of the words of the liturgy. The *Shema* after all, is a prayer service which combines a mental state with a verbal act. M. here tells us that one must recite the words of the *Shema* aloud, carefully, and in the correct order. These rules are attributed to Ushan masters who throughout the tractate define many of the finer details of the obligation to recite the *Shema*.

T. 2:3

A. *One who recites the Shema backwards has not fulfilled his obligation* [M. Ber. 2:3],

B. and so too concerning the [recitation of the] Hallel [Ps. 113-18, recited on festivals], and so too concerning the [recitation of the] Prayer, and so too concerning the [reading of the] Megillah [the Book of Esther, read on Purim].

T. 2:4

A. One who recites the *Shema* and erred by omitting from it one verse should not go back and recite that one verse by itself [cf. M. Ber. 2:3G];

B. rather he begins from that verse and completes [the rest of the paragraph],

C. and so too concerning the [recitation of the] Hallel, and so too concerning the [reading of the] Megillah, and so too concerning the [recitation of the] Prayer.

D. One who entered the synagogue and found that they [the congregation] had [already] recited half [of the *Shema* before he arrived] and completed it with them should not go back and recite [it] from the beginning until that point [at which he had begun reciting with the congregation when he entered];

E. rather he begins from the beginning and [recites] to the end,

F. and so too concerning the [recitation of the] Hallel, and so too concerning the [recitation of the] Prayer, and so too concerning the [reading of the] Megillah.

T. 2:5

A. One who recites the *Shema* and erred, and who does not know where he erred, should go back to the beginning [and recite the whole again] [cf. M. Ber. 2:3].

B. [If] he erred in the middle of a paragraph, he should go back to the beginning of that paragraph.

C. If one errs and skips from the first phrase, 'And you shall write them' [Deut. 6:9] to the second phrase, 'And you shall write them' [Deut. 11:20–and thereby skipped from the first paragraph to the second paragraph], he returns to the first phrase [and recites to the end].

T. provides a number of rulings which supplement M. 2:3F. T. extends M.'s rule to other liturgy–the Hallel psalms recited on the new moon and festival, the Prayer (cf. chapters 4 and 5 below)–and to the recitation of the Book of Esther, on Purim.

T. then adds several related rules about errors in recitation–what to do if while reciting one left out one verse (2:4 A-C), or if one missed part of the recitation in the synagogue (2:4 D-G), or if he knew he erred but did not know where, or if he skipped a section in the recitation (2:5).

2:4

Craftsmen may recite [the *Shema*] from atop a tree or atop a scaffold–something which they are not permitted to do for the [recitation of the] Prayer.

M. appears to shift to a new subject here – recitation of the *Shema* while atop a tree. But in fact this rule relates closely to the central theme of the chapter – the state of mind needed for recitation. Fear, in general, is a distraction which could prevent one from concentrating on prayer. Fear of heights is a common distraction. M., we presume, would not permit a householder to recite while atop a tree since he could not concentrate properly. But the rule before us is much more subtle. The craftsman who is not distracted by heights may recite the *Shema* while high up. M. adds that he may not recite the prayer, since, as we may infer, it requires a deeper kind of concentration which even the craftsman cannot manage while atop a scaffold.

M. then moves on to discuss distractions which disrupt the concentration for recitation. M.'s reference to the prayer here and below in 3:1 adumbrates the concerns of chapters four and five which present the regulations for reciting the Prayer. M. here then turns to two other kinds of distractions, the emotional states of the bridegroom and of the mourner in 2:5 and 3:1 respectively.

T. 2:6

A. Those [scribes] who are writing [Torah] scrolls [i.e. they are like those who study Torah], phylacteries and *mezzuzot*, interrupt [their writing] for the recitation of the *Shema* but do not interrupt for the [recitation of the] Prayer."

B. Rabbi says, "Just as they do not interrupt [their work] for the Prayer, so they do not interrupt [their work] for the recitation of the *Shema*."

C. R. Hanina b. Aqabya says, "Just as they [the scribes] interrupt for the recitation of the *Shema*, so too they interrupt for the [recitation of the] Prayer."

D. Said R. Eleazar b. R. Sadok, "When R. Gamaliel and his court were in Yavneh and preoccupied with communal needs, they did not interrupt [their work] so as not to divert their attention."

T. 2:7

A. The porter–even with his burden on his shoulder, lo, he may recite the *Shema*.

B. But when he is loading or unloading he may not [start to] recite

C. because he cannot concentrate [properly].

D. In any case he may not recite the Prayer until he unloads.

T. 2:8

A. Workers *may recite [the Shema] from atop a tree* [M. 2:4], and they may recite the Prayer from atop an olive tree or from atop a fig tree.

B. But from all other kinds of trees one must come down to recite the Prayer below.

C. And the householder must always come down and recite the Prayer below.

T. 2:9

A. Workers [take time to] recite the *Shema* and recite the blessings before and after it,

B. and eat their bread and recite the blessings before it [the meal] and after it [cf. T. Ber. 5:24],

C. and recite three times daily the Prayer of Eighteen [blessings].

D. But they do not descend before the ark [to lead the recitation of the Prayer in a synagogue].

T. 2:6 A rules that scribes may stop their work temporarily to recite the *Shema*. But since their labor demands intense concentration they remain too distracted to sufficiently turn their minds to prayer. Rabbi and Haninah b. Aqabia disagree with the fine distinction in this case between the *Shema* and the Prayer (C-D). Either one interrupts for neither or for both. A precedent at D that they do not interrupt public service for prayer supports the opinion at B.

The case in 2:7 better parallels our M. 2:4. When the porter is engaged in his work, loading and unloading, he cannot concentrate sufficiently to recite the *Shema*. But when he is just carrying his load he can concentrate and may recite the *Shema* but not the Prayer.

T. 2:8 comments on the kind of tree referred to in our M. 2:4. C makes explicit M.'s assumption that the householder may not recite while atop a tree.

The last pericope in this section is an independent tangential supplement, with little direct relevance here. The regulation is that workers, as a class, may participate in the recitation of liturgy and in the fellowship meal, but may not serve as leaders of the liturgy. Below, at the end of chapter seven, we discuss a related rule, T. 5:24.

2:5

A. A bridegroom is exempt from the recitation of the *Shema* from the first night [after the wedding] until after the Sabbath

B. if he did not consummate the marriage.

C. Once: R. Gamaliel recited [the *Shema*] on the first night after his marriage.

D. His students said to him, "Did our master not teach us that a bridegroom is exempt [from the recitation of the *Shema* on the first night]?"

E. He said to them, "I cannot listen to you. [For I do not wish] to suspend myself from accepting the yoke of the kingdom of heaven [i.e. reciting the *Shema*] even for a short time."

2:6

A. [Gamaliel] bathed on the first night after his wife died.

B. [His students] said to him, "Did not our master teach us that a mourner is forbidden to bathe?"

C. He said to them, "I am not like other men. I am of frail constitution."

2:7

A. When Tabi [Gamaliel's] servant died he accepted condolences on his account.

B. [His students] said to him, "Did you not teach us that one does not accept condolences for slaves?"

C. He said to them, "My slave Tabi was not like other slaves. He was proper."   •

A bridegroom may not recite the *Shema* because until he consummates the marriage, he is distracted by love, lust, fear, or apprehension. The story about Gamaliel which follows tells us that he especially exempted himself from this regulation and recited the *Shema* on his wedding night. Two other stories about Gamaliel round out a triplicate of Gamaliel traditions. The latter two incidents do not relate to the themes of our present chapter.

2:8

A. A bridegroom–if he wishes to recite the *Shema* on the first night [after his wedding]–he may recite.

B. Rabban Simeon b. Gamaliel says, "Not all who wish to take [the liberty of reciting] the name [of God by reciting the *Shema* and its blessings] may do so."

The rule at A reiterates the basis for Gamaliel's actions in the story above at 2:5 C-D. Simeon b. Gamaliel (B) qualifies the law. In some circumstances only exceptional personalities (such as Gamaliel) may recite the *Shema*.

T. 2:10

A. The attendants [at a wedding] and all the members of the wedding party are exempt from [the obligation to recite] the Prayer and from [the obligation to put on] tefillin for the entire seven days [of the wedding celebration].

B. [But] they are obligated to recite the *Shema*.

C. R. Shila says, "The bridegroom is exempt, but all the members of the wedding party are obligated" [cf. M. Ber. 2:5].

T. exempts participants in a wedding from several obligations. We presume that those who celebrate cannot concentrate properly on the Prayer. The gloss at B tells us that they must still recite the *Shema*. But the view at C apparently limits A-B to the bridegroom. Members of the wedding party must fulfill all of their obligations in spite of the festivities.

Chapter Three

BERAKHOT CHAPTER THREE
Additional Rules for the *Shema* and Related Materials

This chapter raises several new issues concerning the practice of reciting the *Shema*. First, what is the rule for mourners and those who participate in a funeral? Must they recite? Or are they exempt because they are too distracted by their grief? This is not a completely new issue, because in fact it continues M.'s concern in the preceding chapter with the importance of concentration in one's recitation.

Mishnah assumes that grief affects the state of mind of the mourner. A grieving person need not recite the *Shema* because he cannot achieve the proper level of concentration. Likewise M. exempts from the recitation of the *Shema* those participants in the funeral who share in the contagion of sorrow. The unit also exempts the mourner from the obligation to wear tefillin, an action usually associated with reciting the Prayer.

The first part of the chapter (3:1-2) serves as a transition. Chapter two discussed the role of concentration in the recitation of the *Shema*. Accordingly, chapter three first takes up the related regulations for the mourner and participants in the funeral, as we explained. Mishnah then turns to rules regarding the obligations of women, slaves and minors for a variety of rituals, including the *Shema*, tefillin, posting the mezuzah, and reciting the blessing after the meal (3:3). Next M. takes up the procedure for the recitation of the *Shema* and meal blessing by one who has suffered a pollution (3:4). Mishnah suggests as an alternative that such a person may meditate for part of the recitation but may not recite the blessings.

The last two units (3:5-6) address several miscellaneous related issues: another rule for the person who suffered a pollution, a regulation for the recitation of the *Shema* by a person who is not dressed, and a rule for its recitation near waste matter. The chapter closes with the question of whether one who suffered a certain kind of pollution must immerse in a ritual bath before reciting the *Shema*.

As a whole, the chapter is loosely knit with no single unifying theme. It is a collection of related miscellanies closing off Mishnah's discussion of the recitation of the *Shema*. By introducing here a few rules for the recitation of the

Prayer, this chapter also serves as a transition to the next major subdivision of the tractate, Chapters Four and Five which deal with rules for the recitation of the Prayer.

In this section T. continues supplementing and expanding M. but adds little new independent material.

3:1

A. He whose deceased relative is lying before him [not yet buried], is exempt from the obligations to recite the *Shema* and to wear tefillin.

B. The [first set of] pallbearers, and the [next people] who replace them, and the [next people] who replace their replacements–whether they go [in the procession to the cemetery] before the bier, or they go behind the bier–

C. If they are needed to [carry] the bier, they are exempt [from reciting the *Shema* and wearing tefillin].

D. And if they are not needed to [carry] the bier, they are obligated [in the *Shema* and tefillin].

E. Both are exempt from [reciting] the Prayer [of Eighteen blessings].

3:2

A. Once they [the mourners] have buried the deceased and returned [from the grave site]–

B. if they have time to begin and complete [the recitation of the *Shema*] before they reach the line [of those who come to console the mourners]–they may begin.

C. And if not–they may not begin.

D. And those who stand in line–the innermost [closest to the mourners] are exempt [from the recitation of the *Shema*] and the outermost are obligated [to recite].

The two parts of this pericope take up distinct but closely related matters. First a mourner need not recite the *Shema* until after his deceased relative is buried (A). Before the funeral, a mourner cannot adequately concentrate on his recitation to achieve the proper state of mind. One may infer that he is also exempt from reciting the Prayer, an act which requires a more intense level of concentration than the recitation of the *Shema*, as we shall see in chapters 4 and 5. Mishnah also exempts him from the obligation of wearing the tefillin, an accouterment of Prayer.

The second part of the pericope (B-E) exempts participants involved directly in the activities of the funeral from the ritual obligations of reciting the *Shema* and wearing tefillin. They are affected most by the contagion of grief, and cannot achieve the proper frame of mind for the recitation. M. exempts even participants who are not essential to the funeral itself from reciting the Prayer (E). Once again, M. proposes higher standards for the Prayer because the Prayer requires a deeper concentration, something a person distracted by a funeral cannot achieve.

M. 3:1 exempts the mourners and some participants in the funeral from the obligation to recite the *Shema* during the service itself. After the funeral is over, they must recite. The first issue of 3:2 (A-C) is whether after the service the mourners must say the *Shema* if the specified time of day for the recitation of the *Shema* has almost passed. M. rules that they must recite if they have sufficient time to do so between the actual burial of the deceased and the moment they return from the grave site to the place where the mourners are consoled (i.e. the line of mourners).

M. 3:2D then elaborates on one element of M. 3:1 above. In addition to those directly involved in the funeral, the folk who come to console the family at the funeral who stand the closest to the mourners, are themselves most directly involved in the proceedings of the funeral, and are thus also exempt from the recitation of the *Shema*. But people who stand a distance away from the mourners are less involved and, hence, obligated to recite.

To review, the first two pericopae of this chapter present rules regarding the obligation to recite the *Shema,* wear tefillin, and recite the Prayer, for mourners, participants in the funeral, and onlookers, in four related units. These regulations for those who grieve at a funeral are related to the laws of the preceding chapter which deal with other situations which affect one's state of mind for prayer.

T. 2:11

A. *Once they [the mourners] have buried the deceased...And...stand in line–*

B. *the innermost [closest to the mourners] are exempt [from the recitation of the Shema]*

C. *and the outermost are obligated [to recite].*

D. R. Judah says, "If they [who came to console the mourners] all were standing in a single line,

E. "those who stand there for the sake of honor [to be first to console the mourners], are obligated [to recite the *Shema*].

F. "[Those who stand there] for the sake of [comforting] the mourner, are exempt [from reciting the *Shema*]."

G. Once they have gone down to [hear the] the eulogy,

H. those who can see the faces [of the mourners] are exempt [from reciting].

I. And those who can not see the faces [of the mourners] are obligated [to recite].

J. The one who eulogizes and all those who participate in the eulogy, may interrupt to recite the *Shema*, but may not interrupt to recite the Prayer.

K. One time the rabbis interrupted [a eulogy] to recite the *Shema* and the Prayer.

The first part of Tosefta (A-F) cites and supplements M. 3:2 A and D. Judah distinguishes among those who come to console the mourner even if they comprise only one line. Tosefta's second part (G-I) adds to Mishnah a related law regarding the obligations of those who attend the eulogy. A third rule (J) concludes the unit. They may interrupt the eulogy to recite the *Shema* but not the Prayer. A precedent (K) contradicts the rule.

3:3

A. Women, slaves and minors are exempt from the [obligation of the] recitation of the *Shema,* and from [wearing] tefillin.

B. And they are obligated in [reciting the] Prayer [of Eighteen blessings],

C. in the [obligation of posting] a mezuzah [on the doorpost],

D. and in [the obligation of reciting] the blessing following the meal.

This unit serves as a short appendix of sorts to the first major subdivision of the tractate, rules for the recitation of the *Shema.* Mishnah's first rule here (A) parallels that of M. 3:1A. M. exempts three categories of persons, women, slaves and minors, from the obligations to recite the *Shema* and wear tefillin. But unlike the mourners in the preceding pericope, M. requires these persons to recite the Prayer (B). In addition M. says that the obligation of these persons extends to other areas as well (C) – putting a mezuzah on a doorpost and reciting the blessings after eating.

With this pericope, Mishnah finishes dealing directly with rules for the recitation of the *Shema.* It turns here to examine several obligations, including among them the obligation to recite the *Shema,* for various cases and categories of individuals. This concern continues for the remainder of the chapter.

3:4

A. One who has discharged semen [in a normal way] may silently meditate [the *Shema*] but may not recite the blessings [because the rabbis deem him to be unclean].

B. Neither [may he recite those blessings] before nor after [the *Shema*].

C. And [regarding the blessings] for the meal—one [who suffered such a discharge] may recite the blessings after it, but may not recite the blessings before it.

D. R. Judah says, "He may recite the blessings before and after [the *Shema* and the meal]."

Any discharge of semen, even in normal intercourse or as a result of a nocturnal emission, brings with it a level of uncleanness decreed by the rabbis. The rabbis bar one who is polluted in this manner from reciting the blessings which frame the *Shema* which the rabbis instituted (A-B). But, M. says, one may meditate over the words of the blessings without speaking them.

The rabbis also prohibit one who discharged semen from reciting the rabbinic blessings before eating. But they do not prevent a person from reciting the blessings one says after eating the meal. As they saw it, those blessings were not decreed on the authority of the rabbis. Rather reciting these blessings was a practice based on the authority of Scripture itself (C).

Judah disagrees with the premise of this regulation. He says normal discharge of semen does not create an uncleanness which can prevent one from reciting blessings. In his view such a person may recite the blessings which frame both the *Shema* and the meal.

T. 2:12

A. One who was ill and discharged semen, upon whom was poured nine קבין of water—

B. [he has purified himself with this action and] behold he may recite.

C. But he cannot exempt others from their obligation [to recite] until he has gone into a pool of forty סאה [of water].

D. R. Judah says, "In either case [he must go into a pool of] forty סאה [even before he may recite for himself]."

E. הזבין and והזבות [those persons who suffer abnormal discharge], והנדות and והיולדות [menstruating women and women after childbirth] may recite from the Torah, Prophets and Writings and may study Mishnah, Midrash, Halakhot and Aggadot.

F. But one who has discharged semen is forbidden [to engage] in all [those activities].

G. R. Yosah says, "He may study routine halakhot but he may not cite [passages from the] Mishnah [lest he become too involved in his study and forget to immerse]."

The first rule of Tosefta (A-C) supplements Mishnah. One who discharged semen because of an illness and who washed in a shower may recite the *Shema* but may not exempt others from their obligations until he undergoes regular purification in a ritual bath. Judah's lemma (D) appears to require the person to undergo a more substantial bathing in a ritual bath, in contrast to his lenient rulings in M. 3:4D and 3:6B. But Lieberman explains the meaning of the rule differently, "One may dip himself in a pool of forty סאה of any kind of water."

The second part of the pericope relates to M. 3:6 below listing activities, including recitation of scripture and study of the rabbinic literature. The four categories of persons mentioned who are unclean because of abnormal discharges may engage in these endeavors. Ironically one who had an ordinary discharge, a lesser form of pollution, may not engage in those activities because of the nature of the rabbinic decree (F). Yosah (G) permits even those who had an ordinary pollution to engage in some form of study.

T. 2:13

A. One who has discharged semen who does not have water [of a miqvah available] to immerse himself in—

B. "Lo, he may recite the *Shema* [to himself] but not out loud, [E. and ed. princeps: and he may not recite the blessings before it or after it,]"

C. the words of R. Meir.

D. And sages say, "He may recite the *Shema* out loud, and recite the blessings before it and after it."

E. Said R. Meir, "Once we were sitting in the house of study in front of R. Aqiba, and we were reciting the *Shema* to ourselves [silently],

F. because a [Roman official] *quaestor* was sitting in the doorway [to observe that they not engage in religious rituals]."

G. They said to him, "One cannot derive a precedent [of law that reciting the *Shema* silently is permissible] from [an incident that occurred in] a time of danger."

This item supplements M. 3:4. M. limits its concern to the blessings before and after the *Shema*. T. discusses the recitation of the *Shema* itself by one who had a seminal discharge. M. accords with the ruling attributed by T. to sages (D). The story at E-G supports sages' view against Meir at C. Ostensibly under one circumstance one may silently meditate over even the scriptural passages of the *Shema* to fulfill his obligation. This applies only in an exceptional case. Ordinarily the law accords with sages (D).

3:5

A. One who was standing and reciting the Prayer [of Eighteen]

B. and remembered that he had discharged semen,

C. should not interrupt [his recitation]

D. but should shorten [the Prayer].

E. One who went down to immerse himself [in a ritual bath]–

F. if he has time to come up [out of the bath] and cover himself and recite [the *Shema*] before the sun rises–

G. he should come up and cover himself and recite.

H. And if not, he should submerge himself [partially] in the water to cover himself and recite.

I. But one may submerge himself neither in foul water, nor in water used for soaking [flax].

J. [And one may not pray near a chamber pot] until one mixes into it [some fresh] water.

K. And how far must one move away from [undiluted urine] and from excrement [before praying]?

L. Four cubits.

A-D of this Mishnah carries forward the preceding concern. One who had an emission who inadvertently started reciting, should recite a shorter version of the Prayer liturgy. The second law (E-H) concerns one who was unclean who went to dip in a ritual bath in the morning. If he has time to dress and then recite the *Shema* before the time for its recitation elapses he should do so. If not, he may recite while unclothed but only if he conceals his nakedness in the murky water. Note that this unit assumes that one must finish reciting before sunrise, contrary to Joshua's rule of M. 1:2E.

A qualification of the rule at H follows at I. One may not recite in proximity to foul water. This idea is picked up in the final rule of the pericope concerning prayer near human wastes. In our translation we interpolated the phrase Maimonides and the other major commentators presumed was missing.

As a whole the rules of the last two pericopae (3:4-5) deal with the theme of purity and the recitation of the liturgy. This section moves from one related rule to another in an appendix to the large subdivision of the tractate, ending with the next Mishnah.

3:6

A. A זב who saw a [seminal] emission, and a נדה who discharged semen, and the woman who had intercourse and then saw a menstrual discharge, must immerse themselves [in a ritual bath to remove the uncleanness caused by the emission or intercourse before they can recite the *Shema*. They must do this even though they remain unclean on account of their more severe condition of uncleanness.]

B. And R. Judah exempts them [from the requirement of immersing themselves because in his view nothing is accomplished through the immersion. They remain unclean by virtue of the more severe uncleanness.]

The preceding M. (3:5) refers to one who had a normal seminal emission. Mishnah extends its interest in this last unit of the chapter to a case of one who suffered an abnormal emission of semen or another kind of discharge. He or she must dip in a ritual pool before reciting the *Shema*. Judah, as above at M. 3:4A, allows such a person to recite even if he or she does not bathe.

T. 2:14

A. One who was standing naked while in the field or while doing his work [when the time came to recite the *Shema*]–

B. behold, this one covers himself with straw or stubble or with anything, and recites [the *Shema*] [cf. M. Ber. 3:5],

C. even though they said, "It is not befitting a man to stand naked,

D. "for when God created man he did not create him naked."

E. As Scripture states, "When I made clouds its [his] garment, and thick darkness its [his] swaddling band" [Job 38:9].

F. "When I made clouds his garment"–this is the fetal sac;

G. "thick darkness his swaddling band"–this is the placenta.

H. One who had an apron of cloth or leather girded around his loins–behold, this one may recite [the *Shema*] [cf. M. Ber. 3:5].

I. Nonetheless one should not recite the Prayer until he covers his heart [i.e., until he is fully dressed].

T. (A-B) extends the second rule of M. 3:5 (E-H) to another case. One who is not clothed may not recite the *Shema* until he covers his nakedness (genitals). C-G says that in general one should not stand naked and adds a scriptural basis for the rule. H provides another related rule for reciting the *Shema* only when clothed. Last, I informs us that for prayer there is a stricter rule. One must wear clothes which cover both the lower and upper portions of the body.

T. 2:15

A. One should not draw his tunic over his head and recite the *Shema* [for in this way he is seeing his naked body].

B. If he had an undergarment girded around him inside [his garments], behold, this is permitted.

C. Two who were sleeping under one cloak are not permitted to recite the *Shema* [since each behold the other's nakedness].

D. But each must cover himself with his [own] clothing and recite [it].

E. But if it was his young son or daughter [under the cloak with him], behold he is permitted [to recite the *Shema*].

Three more rules further supplement the theme of M. 3:5 (E-H), the prohibition against reciting the *Shema* while naked.

T. 2:16

A. A child who is able to eat an olive's bulk of grain [i.e. sufficiently weaned to eat solid foods]–

B. they must move away from his excrement and urine four cubits [before they pray].

C. [Before praying] they move away [four cubits] from human excrement, and [four cubits] from canine excrement

D. if they use [that substance] for tanning hides.

E. A chamber pot–

F. one must stand four cubits away from it [whether it contains excrement or urine before one can recite his prayers].

G. The chamber pot of the bedroom–

H. if one poured some water into it, one may recite [the *Shema*] near it.

I. If not–one may not recite [the *Shema* near it].

J. Rabbi says [E, editio princeps: R. Zakkai says,] "If he put into it a רביעית of water, he may recite [the *Shema*]. If not, he may not recite [the *Shema*]."

K. R. Simeon b. Gamaliel said, "Near the pot in front of the bed one may not recite. Near the pot behind the bed one may recite."

L. R. Simeon b. Eleazar said, "Even in a large house of ten [cubits] by ten [cubits] in which [a chamber pot] was placed, one may not recite unless it [the pot] is covered or placed under the bed."

This pericope supplements M. 3:5K-L, the rule which prohibits recitation of the *Shema* near waste materials. Maimonides' emendation of M. 3:5J reflects T. 2:16. The rules are straightforward.

T. 2:17

A. One should not enter filthy alleyways [soiled with excrement] and recite the *Shema*.

B. Furthermore, even if one entered [the alleyway] while he was reciting [the *Shema*], behold, this one must interrupt [his recitation] until he leaves the vicinity of that place, and [then] he may recite.

T. supplements M. 3:5K-L.

T. 2:18

A. One should not stand to pray [i.e., recite the Prayer] if he needs to relieve himself,

B. as Scripture states, "Prepare to meet your God, O Israel" [Amos 4:12].

2:19

A. One should not urinate where he prays

B. until he has removed himself four אמות [before urinating].

C. One who urinates should not pray in that place

D. until he has removed himself four אמות [before praying].

E. If it [the urine] had dried up or was absorbed [into the ground]–behold, it is permitted [to pray in that place].

These supplements to M. give rules for reciting prayer near waste materials.

T. 2:20

A. One who enters a bath house,

B. [when he stands] in a place where people stand dressed, he may recite the *Shema* or Prayer (Y. has the reading "wear tefillin") there,

C. and it goes without saying that he may extend a greeting there.

D. He may put on his tefillin

E. and it goes without saying that he need not remove them [if he enters wearing them].

F. [When he stands] in a place where most people stand naked,

G. one may not extend a greeting,

H. and it goes without saying that he may not recite the *Shema* or Prayer there.

I. And he must remove his tefillin,

J. and it goes without saying that he may not put them on.

K. [When he stands] in a place where some stand naked and some stand dressed,

L. one may extend a greeting

M. and one may not recite the *Shema* or Prayer.

N. And one need not remove his tefillin,

O. but he may not put them on.

T. 2:21

A. Hillel the Elder says, "Do not appear naked [where others go clothed],

B. "and do not appear clothed [where others go naked],

C. "and do not appear standing [where others sit],

D. "and do not appear sitting [where others stand],

E. "and do not appear laughing [where others weep],

F. "and do not appear weeping [where other laugh],

G. "because Scripture states, '...a time to weep, a time to laugh...a time to embrace, a time to refrain from embracing' [Eccles. 3:4, 5]."

These units are about the proper etiquette for a bathhouse. The *Shema* and Prayer are mentioned as examples of actions which may or may not be performed where people are accustomed to stand naked, hence the pericope is cited here. 2:21 gives a general rule to govern one's etiquette in Hillel's name along with a verse from scripture to justify it. The unit ends with a simple homily.

Chapter Four

Rules for the Prayer of Eighteen Blessings

This chapter introduces a new subject, rules for the recitation of the Prayer of Eighteen blessings. This standard liturgy is in fact nineteen blessings. According to tradition one of the blessings was a later addition. The service is also called the *Amidah,* the prayer recited while standing. Our chapter begins with the question of the time for the recitation, like its parallel counterpart earlier in chapter one, which dealt with the time for saying the *Shema.* Similarly, as we shall see later, the next chapter, chapter five begins with a rule about the concentration needed during recitation of the Prayer, like its parallel counterpart for the *Shema,* above in chapter two.

The Prayer is recited three times on an ordinary day and a fourth time on Sabbaths, holidays and the new moon. Judah, an Ushan, glosses the Mishnah-passages throughout this chapter.

This unit is not tightly constructed around a single central idea. It moves loosely from one rule to another related theme of the recitation of the Prayer. 4:1 spells out the limits of the time period for the recitation of each Prayer. At the outset (4:2-4) the chapter presents several pericopae attributed to Yavneans about various issues related to the Prayer. 4:2 discusses the short prayer for the study hall. Further Yavnean material deals with the form of the Prayer itself in a dispute among three masters (4:3). How many blessings, it asks, make up the Prayer?

The chapter next cites two more Yavnean rulings, one concerning the fixed form of the Prayer, followed by a second about a special prayer to be recited in a dangerous place (4:4).

The section continues with a short unattributed unit on the proper orientation for the Prayer (4:5-6). One must face towards Jerusalem we are told, or if that is not possible, one must think of the Temple during one's recitation of prayer. The segment concludes with a Yavnean ruling glossed by an Ushan concerning the recitation of the Additional Prayer in a public context (4:7). All told, as we indicated, the unit patches together a variety of materials lacking a tight conceptual or thematic unity. It appears that 4:1 and 4:7 serve to frame the chapter's two subunits, 4:2-4 and 4:5-6, all of which deal with the same general topic, rules for the Prayer.

The Yavnean material evinces an understanding of the nature and structure of the Prayer which appears consistent with the early stages in the development of a system of rituals. Most traditional sources and historical analyses locate the origins of the Prayer at Yavneh. Our materials attributed to Yavneans do not contradict this suggestion. They take up such basic questions as the number of component blessings which comprise the Prayer (4:3), whether the Prayer should be fixed at all (4:4), and under what circumstances one must recite the Additional Prayer (4:7). The Ushan unit (4:1), in contrast, suggests that in that era the Prayer was a long-established standardized daily ritual.

The relevant passages in T. develop one of M.'s main themes, i.e. that rules for the recitation of Prayer may be compared with rules for the rituals of the Temple cult (T. 3:1, 3:2, 3:3A). The remainder of the material comments on and supplements M.

T. 3:7 supplies several alternative texts of the "short prayer" to be recited in a place of danger. T. 3:8 gives rules for reciting the Prayer of Sanctification on Sabbaths and festivals, apparently entirely out of context.

T. 3:9 and 3:10-13 are additional independent units which intrude into the present context. 3:9 deals with insertions in the Prayer, the subject of M. 5:2, which it appears to supplement. 3:10-13 supply several attributions which assign to Ushan masters and to the Houses of Hillel and Shammai, rules for special formulas for the Prayer on Sabbath and festivals.

The remainder of the relevant passages in T. supplements M.

4:1

A. The Morning Prayer [may be recited] until midday.

B. R. Judah says, "Until the fourth hour [of the day]."

C. The Afternoon Prayer [may be recited] until the evening.

D. R. Judah says, "Until midafternoon."

E. The Evening Prayer has no fixed rule.

F. And the Prayers of the Additional Service [may be recited] throughout the day.

G. R. Judah says, "Until the seventh hour."

This first pericope lists the latest times of day for the four recitations of the Prayer. The Ushan, Judah, glosses and disputes the times. Standardization of the hours for reciting the Prayer appears to have been a concern of the rabbis at Usha.

4:2

A. R. Nehuniah b. Haqanah used to recite a short Prayer when he entered the study hall and when he exited.

B. They said to him, "What is the nature of this Prayer?"

C. He said to them, "When I enter, I pray that I will cause no offense. And when I exit, I give thanks for my portion."

This section of Yavnean rulings concludes at 4:4. The first rule deals with the short prayer for the study hall. The last item in the brief unit deals with the short prayer to be recited in a place of danger (4:4B-C). A dispute (4:3) and another rule intervene between these materials to round out the unit.

The present ruling is straightforward. One must recite prayers before entering and after leaving the house of study. B-C explains the nature of the prayers. They ask for protection from making an error in interpreting the tradition and give thanks for the opportunity to study the law.

These prayers, however, are only tenuously related to the present context. Up to this point the main concern of the tractate has been the regular cycle of the daily liturgy, the *Shema* and the Prayer of Eighteen. The present tradition deals with special prayers for the occasion of entering and leaving the study hall. Even for the rabbinic Jew who goes to the study hall on a regular daily basis, the prayer upon entering and exiting is of a different nature than that of the regular cycle of the daily liturgy. The former are prayers for protection from harm and for thanksgiving at a specific location and occasion, not recurring daily liturgies. Regulations for the recurring formulae of the daily service resume with the next unit.

T. 3:1

A. Just as the Torah ordained a fixed [time] for the recitation of the *Shema*, so the sages ordained a fixed [time] for the [recitation of the] Prayer.

B. Why did they say, *The morning Prayer [may be recited] until midday* [M. Ber. 4:1A]?

C. For so the daily morning sacrifice was offered until midday.

D. *R. Judah says, "[It may be recited] until the fourth hour"* [M. Ber. 4:1B] [ed. princ. adds: for so the daily morning sacrifice was offered until the fourth hour].

E. Why did they say, *The afternoon Prayer [may be recited] until the evening* [M. Ber. 4:1C]?

F. For so the daily afternoon sacrifice was offered until the evening.

G. *R. Judah says, "Until the mid-afternoon"* [M. Ber. 4:1D] [ed. princ. adds: for so the daily afternoon sacrifice was offered until the mid-afternoon].

And why did they say, *The evening Prayer had no fixed time* [M. Ber. 4:1E]?

For so the limbs and fat pieces were offered all night.

And why did they say, *The additional Prayer [may be recited] all day* [M. Ber. 4:1F]?

For so the additional sacrifice was offered all day.

R. Judah says, "Until the seventh hour" [M. Ber. 4:1G], for so the additional sacrifice was offered until the seventh hour.

And what is [considered] the greater part of the afternoon?

From six and one-half hours onward [i.e., from 12:30 p.m., if daylight is reckoned at 6 a.m.].

H. When is the mid-afternoon?

I. [At] the eleventh hour less a quarter[-hour] [i.e., 4:45 p.m.].

T.'s general observation recognizes that M. 4:1 parallels M. 1:1-2. Both discuss the time period for their respective rituals, the Prayer and the *Shema*. T. explains that the time for the *Shema* was set by the Torah, based on verse from scripture (A), as M. 1:3 indicates. The time for the Prayer was set by the rabbis.

T. next shows that the rabbinic schedule for recitation of the Prayer is based on the schedule which governed the daily sacrifices of the Temple (B-F). As we have seen, the analogy between liturgy and cult is an important theme of the tractate. T. here follows the lead of M. 1:1 and makes explicit the comparison between rules for sacrifice and for prayer.

T. then explains Judah's reference to "mid-afternoon." It assumes that afternoon begins at nine and one half hours after the start of the day, 3:30 on a day when sunrise is a 6:00 A.M. and sunset is at the twelfth hour of the day, at 6:00 P.M. By this reckoning the middle of the afternoon is 4:45, eleven and one half hours into the day.

T. 3:2

A. *The Evening Prayer has no fixed time* [M. Ber. 4:1E]

B. R. Eleazar b. R. Yose says, "[One recites it] at the [time of] the closing of the gates [of the Temple court]."

C. Said R. Eleazar b. R. Yose, "My father would recite it [the Evening Prayer] at the [time of the] closing of the gates."

T. provides a gloss and supporting precedent to suggest a time for the recitation of the Evening Prayer. Once again T. draws an analogy between Prayer and the Temple service. The Evening Prayer should be recited at the time the Temple gates were closed, towards nightfall while it was yet day (cf. Lieberman, *ad. loc.*).

T. 3:3

A. He who recites the Additional Prayer, whether after [the time that] the daily sacrifice was offered or before [the daily time that] the daily sacrifice was offered, has fulfilled his obligation [cf. M. Ber. 4:1].

B. R. Aqiba says, "If one's prayer is fluent, it is a good sign for him. But if not, it is a bad sign for him" [cf. M. Ber. 5:5, M. Ber. 4:3C].

C. He used to say, "One in whom mankind delights, God delights [cf. M. Ber. 5:5; M. Abot 3:10].

D. "One in whom mankind does not delight, God does not delight.

E. "One who is content with his own portion, it is a good sign for him.

F. "One who is not content with his own portion, it is a bad sign for him" [cf. M. Abot 4:1].

T. 3:4

A. Ben Azzai says, "One who is confused about daily matters on account of his wisdom, it is a good sign for him.

B. "If his wisdom was confused by his [preoccupation with] daily matters it is a bad sign for him."

C. He used to say, "One who became physically infirm on account of his [preoccupation with] wisdom, it is a good sign for him.

D. "One who became mentally infirm on account of his preoccupation with worldly matters, it is a bad sign for him."

E. He who recites the Prayer must concentrate [on his prayers] [cf. M. Ber. 5:1].

F. Abba Saul says, "A [Scriptural] allusion to [the requisite act of concentration in] prayer is, 'Thou wilt strengthen their heart, thou wilt incline thine ear' [Ps. 10:17]."

T. first adds a rule which relates to M. 4:1F. It tells us that the Additional Service may be recited throughout the day, whether before or after the time the additional sacrifice was offered in the Temple. B-F then presents an independent homily attributed to Aqiba which continues at 3:4 with a parallel tradition assigned to Ben Azzai. This material begins with a mention of the value of fluency in the recitation of the Prayer, a concern of Aqiba in M.4:3, below.

3:4E-F, out of place here, spells out the assumption of M. 5:1 that one must concentrate during prayer and provides for it a scriptural proof text.

4:3

A. Rabban Gamaliel says, "Each day one must recite a Prayer of Eighteen [blessings]."

B. And R. Joshua says, "[it suffices to recite] an Abstract of Eighteen."

C. R. Aqiba says, "If one is fluent in prayer, he recites a Prayer of Eighteen. And if not, [he recites] an Abstract of Eighteen [blessings]."

Before we explain this M. let us turn to a related text which deals with the origin of the Prayer of Eighteen. The *Amidah*, the Prayer of Eighteen, originated, as tradition has it, with an edict of Gamaliel at Yavneh [T. Babli Meg. 17b]:

A. When did the Prayer [of Eighteen Blessings originate]?

B. It was taught: Simeon of Paqoli established the order of the [Prayer of] Eighteen Blessings before R. Gamaliel at Yavneh.

C. [The Talmud continues with an apparently contradictory tradition:] Said R. Yohanan, and it was also stated as a Tannaitic teaching:

D. It was taught: One hundred and twenty elders, and among them [were] several prophets, ordained the order of the [Prayer of] Eighteen Blessings.

The Talmud manages to harmonize the two conflicting traditions [Babli Meg. 18a]:

A. If "One hundred and twenty elders, and among them [were] several prophets, ordained the order of the Eighteen Blessings," why then did Simeon of Paqoli have to establish [the order of this Prayer also]?

B. [Because the people] forgot the [blessings of the prayer] and he came and established them again.

This tradition indicates that in the Yavnean generation the rabbis sought to institute the regular standardized liturgy of the Prayer of Eighteen Blessings. Yet even though the rabbis sought to institutionalize this effective religious ritual, some resisted the formalization of prayer, claiming that regularization, קבע, diminished the power of the liturgy.

Our materials here in M. relate to the growth of the liturgy. Yavneans masters dispute the form of this nascent and developing Prayer. Gamaliel and Joshua dispute concerning the minimum liturgy required for recitation of the Prayer. Does one need to recite the entire text of eighteen blessings or an abstract of them? Aqiba's compromise subsumes the opinions of both. It appears to be the compelling view and also governs later practice.

T. 3:5

A.   Said R. Judah, "When R. Aqiba would pray with the congregation [in public], he would shorten [his Prayer] more than all of them.

B.   "And when he would pray by himself, one could leave him in one corner [of the room] and find him [later] in another corner,

C.   "on account of his [repeated] bowing and prostration [during his lengthy Prayer]" [cf. M. Ber. 4:3].

Appropriately, T. supplements M. with a tradition concerning Aqiba's own prayer. In public, we are told, he recited less, in private he recited more, bowing and prostrating so much during his lengthy prayer that in the end he would entirely traverse the room.

T. 3:6

A. One might think that you may pray continuously all day long. It was said concerning Daniel, "And he got down upon his knees three times a day [and prayed and gave thanks before his God]" [Dan. 6:10]. (Editio princeps adds: One might think that you can pray facing any direction you wish. [On the contrary,] we learn, "[He went to his house where] he had windows in his upper chamber open toward Jerusalem" [Dan. 6:10].)

B. One might think that they prayed in this way only after they came to the Diaspora. [On the contrary,] we learn, "As he had done previously" [ibid.].

C. One might think that you must raise your voice and pray. It was stated concerning Hannah, "Hannah was speaking in her heart" [I Samuel 1:13].

D. One might think that you may recite the three [daily Prayers] at any time you wish. David already stated, "Evening and morning and noon [I utter my complaint and moan]" [Ps. 55:17].

E. Evening–this is the evening Prayer; morning–this is the morning Prayer; noon–this is the afternoon Prayer.

F. One might think that he may present his petition and [then immediately] depart [from God's presence], Scripture specifies [to the contrary] in the case of Solomon, as it says, "[Yet have regard to the prayer of thy servant and to his supplication, O Lord my God] hearkening to the cry and to the prayer [which thy servant prays before thee this day]" [I Kings 8:28]:

G. the cry–this is the cry [of praise and rejoicing which must accompany petitionary prayer], as it says, "Rejoice in the Lord O ye righteous! Praise befits the upright" [Ps. 33:1];

H. Prayer–this is petition.

I. One does not utter words [of private petition and supplication] after "True and firm" [the blessing recited after the *Shema,* immediately before reciting the Prayer], but he may utter words [of petition] after [reciting] the Prayer [cf. M. Ber. 2:2, T. Ber. 1:2C],

J. even [if the petition is] as [long as] the order of the confession on the Day of Atonement.

The first part of this independent supplement (A-H) supplies Biblical verses to prove that one must pray at specified times of the day (A), that one must pray both in Israel and in the diaspora (B), that one may pray silently (C), that one must recite three separate services (D-E), that one must praise God along with making requests in prayer (F-H). The proof texts draw on the prayers of the Biblical figures Daniel and Hannah, whose actions in their prayers serve as archetypical support for later practice, and rely for support on the Psalms of David, the great master of prayer.

The independent supplement which concludes this unit rules that one may not insert new requests after reciting the *Shema,* but permits a person to make even lengthy additions after reciting the Prayer.

4:4

A. R. Eliezer says, "One who fixes [the recitation of] his Prayer, his Prayer is not supplication."

B. R. Joshua says, "One who goes through a dangerous place should recite a short Prayer, [an Abstract of Eighteen Blessings.]

C. "And he should say, 'God save your people Israel. In all their crises let their needs come before you. Blessed art thou, O Lord who hears our Prayer and supplications."

Eliezer (A) seems to say that one should not recite any prayers with a fixed formula. At face value, Eliezer's view appears to contradict the central notions of the chapter that the time and formula of prayer must be fixed. Therefore most interpreters understand that Eliezer's lemma makes a more subtle point. One should not allow his prayers to become routine, Eliezer says, without new insight or feeling. But no matter how one interprets the saying, it appears to intrude into the unit before us as a singular rule, not well-integrated into its present context.

Joshua rules on yet another matter (B-C). A special protective short prayer may be recited in a dangerous place. As we indicated above, his ruling balances off and concludes this group of Yavnean rulings that starts at 4:2 with the short prayer for the study hall and ends here at 4:4 with the short prayer for a dangerous place, with a dispute and independent lemma on the fixed prayer (4:3-4:4A) in between.

This short chapter is complex because it interjects Yavnean materials on special short prayers into the midst of the discussion of its initial primary subject, the fixed liturgy of the Prayer of Eighteen blessings.

T. 3:7

A. *One who goes through a dangerous place should recite a short prayer* [M. Ber. 4:4B].

B. What is this short prayer?

C. R. Eliezer says, "May thy will be done in the heavens above, and grant ease to those who fear you, and do what is good in thine own eyes. Blessed [art Thou, O Lord,] who hearkens to prayer."

D. R. Yose says, "Hearken to the prayer of thy people Israel and quickly fulfill their requests. Blessed [art Thou, O Lord], who hearkens to prayer."

E. [E, ed. princ.: R. Eleazar b. R. Sadok says, "Hearken to the sound of the cries of your people Israel and quickly fulfill their requests. Blessed [art Thou, O Lord,] who hearkens to prayer."]

F. Others say, "The needs of your people Israel are great and they cannot express them. But let it be your will, Lord our God, and God of our fathers, that you provide for each and every creature his needs, and for each and every person that which he lacks. 'Blessed be the Lord, for he has heard the voice of my supplications' [Ps. 28:6]. Blessed art Thou, O Lord who hears [our Prayer]."

G. Said R. Eleazar b. R. Sadok, "My father used to recite a short prayer on the eve of the Sabbath: 'And on account of the love, Lord our God, with which Thou hast loved thy people Israel, and on account of the compassion, our King, which Thou has bestowed on the members of thy covenant, Thou has given us, Lord our God, this great and holy seventh day with love.'

H. "Over the cup [of wine] he would say, 'who sanctified the Sabbath day,' and he would not conclude [the blessing with a closing benedictory formula]."

T. supplements M.'s rules for special prayers. [T. 3:8-13 are discussed in their most appropriate context, following M. 5:2.]

4:5

A. One who was riding on an ass should dismount [to recite the Prayer].

B. If he cannot dismount he should turn [to face towards Jerusalem].

C. And if he cannot turn, he should direct his thoughts to the chamber of the Holy of Holies [in the Temple of Jerusalem].

4:6

A. One who was travelling on a boat or a raft–he should direct his thoughts to [the chamber of] the Holy of Holies.

This first anonymous pericope (4:5) returns to the theme inaugurated at 4:1, the procedures for the recitation of the Prayer of Eighteen. Correct orientation, facing in the right direction, is a requirement for the recitation of the Prayer. Therefore one must dismount and turn to face Jerusalem before reciting the Prayer. If this is impossible, then one may think of the Temple. Proper thought may substitute for correct orientation. Likewise one who is travelling and cannot discern the direction of Jerusalem (4:6), as a substitute, may direct his thought rather than his posture to the city. Since the role of intention or concentration is usually identified with Ushan rulings, we may assume this set of unattributed rules should be associated with authorities at Usha or thereafter.

T. 3:14

A. A blind man or anyone who is not able to discern directions [whether he faces east or west,] lo, they pray [by turning their thoughts] towards their Father in heaven.

B. As it says, "And they pray to the Lord [toward the city which thou hast chosen and the house which I have built for thy name]" [I Kings 8:44].

T. extends M.'s rule about one who cannot tell which direction is Jerusalem. According to T. in such a situation one may direct his prayers to heaven by facing heavenward and with the proper thoughts. A phrase from Scripture proves the point.

T. 3:15

A. Those who stand [and pray] outside the Land of Israel, turn to face the Land of Israel [to pray].

B. As Scripture states, "And they pray to thee toward their land which thou gavest their fathers" [II Chron. 6:39, cf. I Kings 8:48].

C. Those who stand [and pray] in the Land of Israel turn to face Jerusalem.

D. As Scripture states, "Toward the city which thou hast chosen" [II Chron. 6:34].

T. 3:16

A. Those who stand [and pray] in Jerusalem, turn to face the Temple.

B. As Scripture states, "And the house which I have built for thy name" [II Chron. 6:32].

C. And those who stand [and pray] in the Temple, turn to face the chamber of the Holy of Holies.

D. As Scripture states, "[And hearken to the supplication of thy servant and of thy people Israel,] when they pray toward this place; [yea, hear thou in heaven thy dwelling place; and when thou hearest, forgive]" [I Kings 8:30].

E. It turns out that [when they pray] those who stand north [of the Temple], face south, those who stand in the south, face north, those who stand in the east, face west, those who stand in the west, face east.

F. It turns out all of Israel prays towards one place.

T. 3:17

A. One should not stand to pray on top of a bed, or on a bench or a chair, or in any elevated place,

B. for there may be no elevation [or haughtiness] before God,

C. as it is written, "Out of the depths I cry out to thee, O Lord" [Ps. 130:1].

D. But if he was elderly or ill, it is permitted [to recite prayers on top of a bed or in a chair, or other elevated place].

T. 3:18

A. *One who was riding on an ass—*

B. if there is someone who can hold the ass [while he prays so that it will not run away], he should dismount and pray.

C. If not, he prays where he is [mounted upon the animal].

D. Rabbi says, "In either case he should pray where he is

E. for that way his mind is more at ease [and he can better concentrate]."

T. 3:19

A. One who arose early to go on a journey—

B. lo, he may take a shofar and blow it, [take] a lulab and wave it, take the scroll [of Esther, on Purim] and read from it [before he leaves his house],

C. but when the time comes for the recitation of the *Shema,* he must recite it [where he is, even if already on the road].

D. One who arose early to travel in a wagon or on a boat—

E. lo, he recites the Prayer [before he departs],

F. but when the time comes for the recitation of the *Shema,* he must recite it [where he is, even if already traveling].

T.'s point at 3:15-16 is that all must face toward Jerusalem when reciting the Prayer. 3:17 supplements M. 4:5. One must dismount before praying, even if facing in the proper direction toward Jerusalem, because Prayer may not be recited by one who is elevated off the ground.

3:18 cites and further supplements M. 4:5. By dismounting the animal one may become distracted for fear that his animal may bolt and run away while he stands to pray. One should dismount only if someone can hold the beast for him while he recites his prayer. Rabbi's gloss suggests that one will be distracted even if someone can hold the animal for him. He should therefore preferably recite while upon his mount.

M.'s mention of the prayer of a person who is travelling is the primary concern of T. 3:19. This unit deals with the obligation of the traveller to pray and to fulfill certain other rituals. The traveller who awakens early to go out on the road must first fulfill those commandments which he may not be able to properly fulfill on the journey (e.g. taking the lulab, blowing the shofar, reading the scroll) because he will not have the object available to perform the ritual. He should delay his recitation of the *Shema* until the proper time, even if he will be out on the road at that hour, since he has no need for any special object to fulfill that obligation.

D-F is more closely associated with our M. One who gets up early to go out and travel on a boat must first recite the Prayer. The underlying assumption is that once the person is out on the boat he will not be able to discern the direction for his Prayer. One may wait until later when on the boat to recite the *Shema* since for that recitation one need not be concerned about the direction he faces. As evident, T.'s rule supplements and extends M.'s concern.

4:7

A. R. Eleazar b. Azariah says, "The Additional Prayer is said only with the
חבר עיר [congregation or association of the town]."

B. And sages say, "Both with the חבר עיר and not with the חבר עיר."

C. R. Judah said in his [Eleazar's] name, "Any place where there is a חבר עיר
[i.e. a place where they recite the Prayer in public] an individual is exempt from
[reciting] the Additional Prayer."

This last pericope is an independent addition to the first unit of the chapter
which mentions the Additional Prayer (4:1F-G), said on Sabbaths, holidays, and
new moons. According to Eleazar they only recite this prayer in public with the
congregation. Sages disagree. One may say it either with the congregation, in
public, or apart from the congregation, in private. Judah's rule appears to
present a compromise between the two positions. Wherever there is a
congregation, the individual is exempt from his obligation. He recites in public
with the congregation. In other cases we presume he may recite in private.
Thus this issue concerning the procedure for the recitation of the Additional
Prayer, initially addressed in a ruling attributed to a Yavnean, Eleazar, is settled
by Judah, an Ushan.

This diverse chapter closes with this ruling. We turn in the next chapter to
some rules pertaining to the definition of the state of mind which must
accompany the recitation of the Prayer.

Chapter Five

BERAKHOT CHAPTER FIVE
Additional Rules for the Prayer

This chapter opens with a definition of the frame of mind one must have for reciting the Prayer of Eighteen, the *Amidah*. To recite the Prayer one must have a "solemn frame of mind (5:1A)." The authorities behind Mishnah knew, as we saw in chapter two, that it is difficult to define in positive terms the nature of a frame of mind. Accordingly, our text indirectly describes the nature of the concentration needed during the Prayer as it did for the *Shema* earlier in chapter two.

Mishnah says that during the recitation of the Prayer one should shut out all forms of distraction even if by so doing he puts himself in the mortal danger of a serpent's sting or a king's wrath (5:1C).

Earlier, we recall, M. defined the nature of the concentration needed for the recitation of the *Shema* (M. 2:1) in terms of limiting the exchange of greetings with others. M.'s point there was that while reciting the *Shema*, one has to shut out some forms of social exchange and concentrate on his recitation. Likewise Mishnah rules here that during the recitation of the Prayer, through concentration, one must further close down his awareness of the surrounding world.

The chapter does not dwell on this subject for long. It moves rapidly on to other regulations for the recitation of the Prayer. 5:2 presents several laws on the insertion of special formulae into the Prayer liturgy: the phrases which invoke prayers for rain, inserted in the winter season (A-B), and the verses which make up the Prayer of Division, to be added at the conclusion of the Sabbath (C-E).

The final three pericopae of the chapter move away from the rules for sanctioned additions to the liturgy. They first deal with the flip side of this subject, rules regarding improper insertions into the Prayer (5:3A). Then M. turns to the related issue of what to do if one errs during recitation of the Prayer (B-E). This unit, along with 5:4 and 5:5, form a loose triplicate on the theme of errors in the recitation of the Prayer. As we shall see, that item and the following two pericopae assume that these rules apply to a public context where a leader, selected by the congregation, "goes before the ark" to recite the Prayer.

It appears to take for granted that the Prayer will be recited in a collective setting such as a synagogue.

M.'s interest in the subject of errors in recitation by the leader brings it to a related issue (5:4). What does the leader do when the priests recite their blessing during his recitation of the Prayer? And what does the leader do if he is the only priest in the congregation? Does he recite the priestly blessing in the middle of his recitation of the Prayer?

The chapter concludes with some general observations (5:5). Prayer may serve as an omen. If one recites his prayer fluently it is a good sign. If he makes mistakes it is a bad sign. Furthermore the errors made by a leader are a portent for the congregation. The concluding story about Haninah ben Dosa makes a related point. The prayers a rabbi recites for a sick person may serve as signs about that person's chance of recovery. Haninah says that if the prayers which he recited on behalf of a person were fluent he knew they were accepted and the patient would recover. If not, it was a bad sign for the sick person.

This chapter lacks a single principal unifying theme. Its rules deal loosely with several distinct aspects of the recitation of the Prayer: the concentration one must have, special changes for the liturgy, errors in reciting and their ramifications. We may however infer from these rules some important facts about early rabbinic prayer.

First, there is further indication in the rules of 5:2, attributed to Yavneans concerning the special adaptations of the liturgy, that the regulated structure of collective public rabbinic prayer first took formal shape in that generation. Next from 5:3 we may infer, as we said, that the rabbis assumed that the Prayer was a communal ritual recited by a leader selected by a congregation to go before the ark as their agent. Then from 5:4 we may deduce that another ritual, the priestly blessing, was combined with the recitation of the Prayer and that there was some concern over the implementation of the two together. Since these last materials are anonymous, the best we can say is that they represent assumptions no later than the generation of the redactor of M.

The last item in the chapter assumes that one may interpret his fluency, or lack thereof, of one's recitation of the Prayer as an omen. This tradition is illustrated with a story about a Yavnean rabbi who in other rabbinic traditions evinced wondrous powers. This point has clear homiletical value but does not tell us much about the origins or development of the liturgy. With this related miscellany, M. closes its units on prayer and turns somewhat abruptly in the next chapter to the wholly new issue of blessings for foods.

The pertinent passages in T. first directly supplement M.'s interest in the nature of the concentration needed for the recitation of the Prayer. T. follows this with material dealing with special insertions in the Prayer and meal blessing for a mourner (3:23-24). Here we also cite previous passages (T. 3:8- 13), pertinent to this context. T. concludes with a single unit regarding other special insertions in the Prayer.

5:1

A. One may stand to pray only with a solemn frame of mind.

B. The ancient saints used to tarry for a while, and then pray so that they could first direct their thoughts [to God].

C. [One who is praying,] even if a king extends to him a greeting, he should not respond; even if a serpent is coiled to strike at his heel, he should not interrupt [his recitation].

One who prays must have a serious disposition, a solemn frame of mind, as M. in A puts it (literally, a respectful or heavy mind). B and C indirectly explain A's rule. B first remarks that one needs to prepare himself for entering the right state of mind for prayer, to direct one's thoughts to God. It may not be immediately clear how one is to do this. M. then explains in C, in one tightly compacted line, that a person must completely shut out from his mind all external distractions in achieving and maintaining the consciousness needed for the recitation of the Prayer. A person should concentrate so intensely that even if faced with mortal danger he should not interrupt his Prayer.

This short pericope serves as the counterpart to the material in Chapter Two which deals with the state of mind one needs to achieve for the recitation of the *Shema* (2:1). Recall that there M. spoke of the need to direct one's thoughts as it does in the present pericope. One who had the proper intention while reciting the verses of the *Shema* from the Torah could fulfill his obligation to recite the *Shema*. The same Hebrew root is used in both places, כון, literally to direct (one's thoughts). Also, Mishnah earlier used the example of an interruption for extending a greeting to illustrate in more concrete and direct terms the nature of the concentration one must have for reciting the *Shema* (2:1D-G).

Here in our unit, Mishnah speaks in terms of much more serious and threatening distractions which one still should not permit to invade his consciousness during his recitation of the Prayer (5:1C). M. adds here that one must spend some time in preparation for the recitation of the Prayer to achieve the proper state of mind as did the ancient saints (5:1B). By contrast to the Prayer, the recitation of the *Shema* is a less formal and demanding ritual.

T. 3:20

A. If one was standing and praying in a wide street or a public place,

B. lo he may move aside to let an ass or a wagon pass, as long as he does not interrupt [his Prayer].

C. They said concerning R. Haninah b. Dosa that while he was standing and praying, a poisonous lizard bit him, but he did not interrupt [his Prayer].

D. They went and found [the lizard] dead at the entrance to its hole.

E. They said, "Woe to the person who is bitten by the lizard. Woe to the lizard who bit R. Hanina Ben Dosa."

M. 5:1C deals with the distractions which one must shut out during his recitation of the prayer. T. A-B adds to this that one may move aside during his recitation of prayer in a public thoroughfare to let traffic pass as long as he does not stop reciting.

The story at C-D illustrates how the action of Ben Dosa, considered by the rabbis to be a virtuoso of prayer, accorded with M.'s principle that one must not interrupt the prayer even if faced with mortal danger. He ignored a poisonous lizard, it bit him, and the lizard died. Ben Dosa was protected by his recitation of the Prayer.

T. 3:21

A. *One may stand to pray* neither after conversation, nor after laughter, nor after levity, but only after words of wisdom [i.e. Torah].

B. And likewise one may depart from his associate neither after conversation, nor after laughter, nor after levity, but only after words of Torah.

C. For so we find that the ancient prophets concluded their messages with words of praise and consolation.

T. further defines the "solemn frame of mind" of M. 5:1A. It means that one must have a serious attitude before he prays. That can be achieved by speaking words of wisdom. It certainly cannot be reached out of levity, laughter, or idle conversation. B-C extend T.'s point.

T. 3:22

A. If one was writing God's name [in a Torah scroll],

B. *Even if a king extends to him a greeting, he should not respond.*

C. If one was writing five or six consecutive divine names [such as El, Elohim, Yahweh] lo, he should finish writing one and return the greeting.

Other activities require the same state of mind as M. demands for the recitation of the Prayer. A scribe who writes Torah scrolls must concentrate intensely while he writes the name of God. T. uses M.'s phrase in describing the kinds of distractions which the scribe must ignore – even the greeting of a king.

[T. 3:23-5 are discussed following M. 5:5. T. 3:26 cites M. 8:8.]

5:2

A. They mention the [liturgical formula which deals with the] "Wonders of the rains" [i.e. "Who causes the winds to blow and the rain to fall" during the rainy season] in [the second blessing of the Prayer of Eighteen, called] "The Resurrection of the Dead."

B. And they [add during the winter the phrase, "Grant us dew and rain for blessing," to] ask for rain in [the ninth blessing, called] "The Blessing of the Years."

C. And [they insert] the Prayer of Division [recited at the conclusion of a Sabbath or Festival day] in [the fourth blessing of the Prayer of Eighteen on Saturday night, called] "Endower of Knowledge."

D. R. Aqiba says, "One says it as a separate fourth blessing."

E. R. Eliezer says, "[One inserts it] in the 'Thanksgiving,' [the name of the eighteenth blessing of the prayer of Eighteen]."

A mention of the wonders of the rains is inserted in the Prayer during the rainy season from Shemini Aseret in the fall until Passover in the spring (cf. M. Ta'anit 1:13). The request for rains is added in the winter from early December until Passover. M. says that one adds the phrase about the rains ("He who causes the winds to blow and brings down the rains") in the second blessing of the Prayer (A) and they add the formula of the request for rains ("And grant dew and rain for blessing") in the ninth blessing (B).

C-E speak of the Prayer of Division formula which must be recited in the Prayer of the Saturday night evening service. The Yavneans dispute the proper place for this insertion, an additional indication that the liturgy was not completely formalized in this generation, as we noted above.

T. 3:8

A. [If, on the Sabbath or festival, one has only enough wine to drink at one meal] in honor of the day or in honor of the eve [of the Sabbath or festival], the honor of the day takes precedence over the honor of the evening [viz., he should drink the wine at the daytime meal].

B. If he has [enough wine for] only one cup, [the blessing dealing with] the sanctification of the day [recited over a cup of wine at the outset of the Sabbath or festival] takes precedence over the [meal in] honor of the day and the [meal in] honor of the eve [of the Sabbath or festival, viz., he drinks the wine before either meal has begun].

C. On the eve of the Sabbath and the eve of the festivals sanctification of the day is to be [recited] over the cup [of wine], and sanctification of the day is to be [recited] in the grace after meals.

D. On the Sabbath [day], and festival [days], the new moon, and the intermediate days of the festivals, sanctification of the day is to be [recited] in the grace after meals, but sanctification of the day is not to be [recited] over the cup [of wine].

T. 3:9

A. If one did not mention the mightiness of [God's deeds in causing] the rains [to fall] in [the second blessing of the Prayer, which deals with] the resurrection of the dead,

B. or if one did not petition for rainfall in the blessing for the years [viz., the ninth blessing of the Prayer, the petition for a fruitful and prosperous year],

C. they make him begin [reciting the entire Prayer] again.

D. If he did not recite the Prayer of Division [acknowledging the distinctiveness and sanctity of the people Israel and the Sabbath day] in [the fourth blessing, which concludes,] "gracious giver of knowledge," he may recite it over a cup [of wine; cf. M. Ber. 5:2].

E. If he did not recite it [even at that time], they make him begin [the Prayer] again.

F. [ed. princ.: R. Yose says, "So too, if one did not mention the covenant [between God and Israel; later liturgical rites mention here the covenant of circumcision] in the blessing of the Land [i.e., the third blessing in the grace after meals], they make him begin [the Prayer] again."]

T. 3:10

A. Any [minor holiday] on which the Additional Prayer is not recited,

B. such as Hanukkah and Purim,

C. in the morning and afternoon one recites eighteen [blessings; viz., the number of blessings recited in the Prayer on ordinary days], and recites [among their number a prayer] appropriate to the occasion.

D. If he did not recite this [prayer], they do not make him begin [the Prayer] again.

E. All [minor holidays] on which the Additional Prayer [is recited],

F. such as the new moon and the intermediate days of the festival,

G. in the morning and afternoon one recites eighteen [blessings in the Prayer] and recites [among their number a prayer dealing with] the sanctity of the day to be included in the [blessings concerning the Temple] service.

H. *R. Eliezer says, "[It is included] in the Thanksgiving [blessing]"* [M. Ber. 5:2].

I. If he did not recite it, they make him repeat [the Prayer] again.

J. And in the Additional Prayer [on those days] one recites seven [blessings in the Prayer] and recites [a separate blessing concerning] the sanctity of the day in the middle [as the fourth blessing].

T. 3:11

A. [Concerning] a Sabbath which fell on the New Moon or during the intermediate days of a festival—

B. in the morning and afternoon one recites seven [blessings in the Prayer] and recites [a prayer dealing with] the sanctity of the day in the [blessing concerning the Temple] service [V: in the middle].

C. *R. Eliezer says, "[It is included] in the Thanksgiving [blessing]."*

D. If he did not recite it, they make him repeat [the Prayer] again.

E. And in the Additional Prayers one recites seven [blessings in the Prayer] and recites the [blessings concerning] the sanctity of the day in the middle [i.e., as the fourth blessing].

T. 3:12

A. On the Sabbath and on festivals and on the Day of Atonement one recites seven [blessings in the Prayer] and recites the [blessing concerning] the sanctity of the day in the middle [as the fourth blessing].

B. Rabban Simeon b. Gamaliel and R. Ishmael b. R. Yohanan b. Beroqah say "Any time one must [recite] seven [blessings], he recites the [blessing concerning the] sanctity of the day in the middle."

T. 3:13

A. [Concerning] the festival day of the New Year which fell on the Sabbath,

B. the House of Shammai say, "One recites ten [blessings in the Prayer],"

C. and the House of Hillel say, "One recites nine [blessings in the Prayer]."

D. [Concerning] a festival day which fell on the Sabbath—

E. the House of Shammai say, "He recites eight [Blessings in the Prayer] and recites [the blessing] concerning the Sabbath separately and [the blessing] concerning the festival separately, and he recites [the blessing] concerning the Sabbath, first."

F. And the House of Hillel say, "He recites seven [blessings in the Prayer], he begins [the fourth blessing] with [mention of] the Sabbath and concludes with [mention of] the Sabbath and mentions the sanctity of the day [i.e., the festival] in the middle."

G. Rabbi [E, ed. princ.: R. Nathan] says, "Also: he concludes it [the fourth blessing, with a benedictory formula:] 'Praised [be Thou, O Lord," who sanctifies the Sabbath, Israel, and the festivals.'"

3:8 appears here because it deals with special insertions for the Prayer on the Sabbath. In T. it follows the reference to Sadok's practice of reciting a formula over the cup of wine he drank on the eve of the Sabbath (T. 3:7). 3:8 now gives us a short unit on the priorities for one who has only a limited amount of wine. Given a choice between drinking it at a meal during the night or during the day, one must drink it during the day. On the Sabbath one must use his wine first for the Prayer of Sanctification, before he may use it for a meal (B).

C-D then elaborates on the practice of reciting the Prayer of Sanctification. On the eves of Sabbaths and festivals they recite the Prayer of Sanctification over a cup of wine before the meal and they insert an allusion to the Sabbath day in the blessings which follow the meal. On the Sabbath and festival day itself, they insert an allusion to the sanctity of the day only in the blessings after the meal. They do not recite a special Prayer of Sanctification over a cup of wine before the daytime meal begins on the Sabbath or festival, or before any meal on the new moon or the intermediate days of the festival.

3:9 best supplements M. 5:2 as we have located it. C rules that one who did not insert the formula for the Prayer of Division in the Prayer of Eighteen in the evening at the conclusion of the Sabbath may recite the formula over a cup of wine. If he forgets and omits this as well, he must go back and recite it. Related to this is the rule of Yose (F) which adds that one must go back and repeat if he omits the mention of the covenant in the second blessing after the meal. T. thus continues its theme with further rules for one who accidentally omits special additions he is supposed to make to the Prayers and blessings.

The main issues of 3:10 are where in the Prayer does one insert references to special occasions, and what to do if one forgets to insert a special formula. Does he have to repeat the entire liturgy in order to recite the short reference to the special occasion? The unit rules that on those days when no Additional Service is recited, one makes a special insertion for the occasion in the Prayers. If one forgets to recite this in the liturgy, he need not go back to repeat the Service (A-D). On those days when they also recite the Additional Prayer, one inserts a special formula in the Morning and Afternoon Prayers. If he forgot to recite this, he must repeat the service. One also recites a special form of the liturgy for the Additional Prayer–seven blessings instead of the usual eighteen, with the middle blessing reserved for the references to the special sanctity of the day.

3:11-13 complete the discussion of rules for modifying the Prayer on special occasions. 3:11 addresses the more complicated issue of the composition of the liturgy on several unusual sacred days. When the new moon falls on the Sabbath, for instance, one recites the Prayers as usual for the Sabbath but adds a special insertion for the new moon. T. tells us where one must insert those references in the Morning, Afternoon, and Additional Prayers. 3:12 adds a general rule, taken for granted in the preceding, that the Prayers of the Sabbath, festival and Day of Atonement consist of seven rather then eighteen blessings and the reference to the Sanctity of the day itself is to be found in the middle blessing. T. attributes this latter rule to Ushans, suggesting that this entire section may stem from that period. If so, the glosses of Eliezer at 3:10H and 3:11C may have been artificially affixed to the unit on the basis of his lemma in M. 5:2E.

3:13 gives us pause in assigning this entire section to a later period of development. It cites two Houses' disputes regarding the structure of the Prayers for the New Year and the festival which coincide with the Sabbath. The Houses disagree over the number of blessings one recites in such instance. Does one combine the blessing for the sanctity of the Sabbath together with the blessing for the sanctity of the New Year's day or festival day, or does he recite them as separate blessings. Rabbi's rule at G indicates that, as we expected, the law follows the Hillelites. The blessings are combined, and the closing formula is altered to fit the occasion.

There is no reason to dismiss these latter disputes as artificial anachronisms of a later generation. While the consensus of the evidence and the tradition leads us to conclude that formalized daily prayer takes root at Yavneh, there is no reason to insist that regular prayers for special occasions were unknown prior to that time in the generation of the Houses.

5:3

A. They silence one who says [in leading the Prayer of Eighteen], "May thy mercy reach [even] the nest of a bird," or "May thy name be invoked for the good," or "We give thanks, we give thanks." [These are not sanctioned liturgical formula, because they have heretical overtones.]

B. He who goes before the ark [to lead the recitation of the Prayer of Eighteen] and erred, they replace him with another.

C. And one may not decline at that time [if asked to replace the one who errs].

D. Whence does [the replacement] begin [to recite]?

E. From the beginning of the blessing in which [the previous leader] erred.

Most commentators follow the Talmudic explanation and stress that the formulae listed in A are improper insertions into the Prayer because they represent heretical beliefs or questionable theological implications about the mercy of God, the goodness of God, or the unity of God. (Cf. M. Megillah 4:9, B. Ber. 33B.)

B-E takes up a related question. What do they do if the leader errs (e.g. by reciting the wrong phrase) in the recitation of the Prayer? B-C tells us that he is replaced with another from the congregation. D-E goes on to a concern secondary to the preceding. At what point do they begin reciting after replacing the leader? Does the new leader start again from the beginning of the Prayer? E rules that he may begin from the place at which the previous leader made the error.

These rules take a certain context for granted. The Prayer is recited by an intercessor for the congregation in a public setting. By way of contrast recall that no such background is expected for the recitation of the *Shema*. Our sources suggest that each recites the *Shema* for himself either individually or in a collective setting (cf. M. chapters 1 and 2, and esp. T. 2:4).

5:4

A. He who goes before the ark [to lead the Prayer of Eighteen] shall not answer "Amen" after the [blessing recited by the] priests [in the eighteenth blessing of the Prayer of Eighteen].

B. Because of the confusion [which might arise by virtue of engaging in such an act].

C. And if [the leader] is the only priest present [at the service], he should not raise his hands [to recite the Priestly Blessing].

D. But if he is sure that he can raise his hands [to recite the blessing] and return to his [recitation of the] Prayer [of Eighteen without becoming confused], he is permitted [to raise his hands].

M. includes this tangential unit here because it carries forward somewhat M. 5:3's interest in rules about errors in the recitation of the Prayer. The priests recite the verses from Numbers 6:24-6, Aaron's priestly blessing, during the recitation of the Prayer. A-B says that the leader may not respond "Amen" to these blessings lest he become confused and make an error.

C-D raises a secondary issue. If the leader who recites the Prayer is the only priest in the congregation, may he interrupt his recitation and recite the priestly blessing? If he is confident that he can recite the priestly blessing and then return and complete his recitation of the Prayer, D says, he may go ahead and bless the people.

5:5

A. He who recites the Prayer and erred, it is a bad sign for him.

B. And if he is an agent of the congregation [to lead the Prayer], it is a bad sign for them that appointed him.

C. [The principle is that] a person's agent personifies him [i.e. stands in his stead].

D. They said concerning R. Haninah b. Dosa that he used to pray for the sick and could say who would live and who would die.

E. They said to him, "Whence do you know?"

F. He said to them, "If my prayer is fluent, then I know it is accepted.

G. "And if not, then I know it is rejected."

M. underscores the importance of correctly reciting the Prayer because an error is a inauspicious sign. If the leader of the Prayer errs it is a bad indication for the entire congregation (A-C).

The concluding story about Ben Dosa, a virtuoso of prayer, illustrates how one rabbi interpreted his fluency or errors in reciting his special prayers on behalf of a person who was ill. If his prayer was not fluent it was a unfortunate omen for the sick person. (Also cf. T. 3:20 discusses above concerning Ben Dosa's powers of prayer.)

T. 3:23

A. [In] a locale where it is customary to recite the blessing for mourners as three [separate blessings], they recite three; [where it is customary to recite] two–they recite two; [where it is customary to recite] one–they recite one.

T. 3:24

A. [In] a locale where it is customary to recite the blessing for mourners as three [separate blessings in the grace after meals]–

B. he inserts the first in [the blessing concerning] the resurrection of the dead [the invitational formula of the grace after meals; so Lieberman, TK, I, p. 51] and concludes it [with the words], "he who resurrects the dead."

C. [He inserts] the second in [blessing concerning] comforting the mourners [a form of the third blessing in the grace after meals] and concludes it [with the words], "He who comforts his people in his city."

D. [He inserts] the third in [the blessing concerning] acts of loving recompense [the fourth blessing of the grace after meals] and does not conclude [the blessings with a closing formula].

E. He who delivers a funeral address in a cemetery does not conclude [the blessing with a closing benedictory formula].

The relationship of these pericopae to the present context is at best tangential. T. includes this independent supplement because it speaks of the insertion which they make in the prayer in the house of mourning. T. 3:23 says the practice of a mourner reciting special blessings varies from place to place. 3:24 then gives us only the specifics for the first alternative listed by T., the practice of reciting three blessings. B tells us that they insert a special formula in the second blessing of the prayer. That is the first of the "mourner's blessings." They also modify two of the blessings of the meal (C-D). E concludes with a miscellaneous rule regarding the funeral.

T. 3:25

A. "The eighteen blessings of which the sages spoke correspond to the eighteen invocations [of God's name in Psalm 29]: 'Ascribe to the Lord.'

B. They insert the references to the heretics in the blessing concerning the slanderers [the twelfth],

C. and the references to [the elders and] the proselytes in the blessing concerning the righteous [the thirteenth],

D. and the reference to [the restoration of the monarchy of] David in the blessing concerning the rebuilding of Jerusalem [the fourteenth].

E. If he recited each of them separately [as independent blessings], he still fulfilled his obligation.

A provides a scriptural basis for the original eighteen blessings of the Prayer. B-E discusses various special references in the blessings of the Prayer.

[T. 3:26 cites M. 8:8, see below.]

Chapter Six

BERAKHOT CHAPTER SIX
Blessings for Foods

With this chapter M. begins a new topic, regulations regarding the blessings for the rabbinic Jew to recite before eating any food. Chapters Seven and Eight continue on related themes with rules for the blessings after eating and for other procedures at the meal.

The subject matter of the remainder of the tractate is thematically distinct from that of the first five chapters of Berakhot. But the topics are linked together through at least one important common bond. M. throughout is concerned with rules regarding the blessing, the shared basic formulaic component of the liturgy which frames the *Shema* (chapters 1-3), which constitutes the basic building block of the liturgy of the Prayer (chapters 4-5), and, in the present context (Ch. 6), which comprises the formula that one recites before eating.

The present chapter presumes that the rabbinic practice of reciting blessings transforms the formal dinner, the less formal occasional meal, and every other occasion of eating, into religious rituals.

The rabbis require the Jew to recite a short blessing before eating and a more substantial liturgical prayer, made up of longer blessings, after the dinner or meal. M. sees no reason to spell all this out since it presumes that every adult Jew knows what basic blessings to recite before and after eating. The rules here deal only with some of the more subtle issues of reciting food blessings.

M. first gives us a simple taxonomy of blessings for the different categories of foods (6:1). Produce of trees, that is fruit, and produce of the ground, that is vegetables, are the two main groups. Bread and wine, the staple foods of the Israelite diet, have their own unique blessings. But salad greens do not, except according to Judah (6:1G). All other foods, such as milk, cheese, and eggs, fall into another general category with its own blessing (6:3A). Interestingly, meat is not mentioned at all. Most likely it was not a prominent part of the average Jew's basic diet. The first concern of M. then is the categorization of foods and the assignment of a blessing for each category.

The second concern is the regulation of the correct and efficient use of these food blessings. M. raises questions about the consequences of reciting the wrong blessing over a food (6:2). Is it effective or must one who errs recite its regular blessing? Can one blessing serve several types of foods in the context of a meal? If so which blessing does one recite (6:4-5)? If one eats the same food at several times during a dinner, does the first blessing suffice for all occasions (6:5)?

Other questions follow. Can one person recite a blessing on behalf of others who eat together with him? At what stages of the dinner must one recite his own blessing (6:6)? Also is there a general rule for a blessing over one food which is secondary to another (6:7)? Finally, what blessings are recited after the meal (6:8)?

This unit gives us little potential historical data mainly due to its limited attributions and attestations. Judah glosses at several points in the chapter (6:1G, 6:3C, and at 6:4B–as party in a dispute). One enigmatic gloss is attributed to the House of Shammai (6:5E). Two Yavneans, Aqiba and Tarfon, appear in the last pericope. On this scant evidence of the attributions the most we can say is that the system of blessings recited before eating seems to have been known at Usha, the character of the blessings after the meal was an issue at Yavneh, and some notions of blessings before eating may have been the subjects of rulings in the first century.

One thematic concern which links together many of the issues of the chapter is that one must make economical use of blessings. Where one blessing suffices, there is no need to recite two. Where a blessing recited by one person is enough, a second person need not recite. What motivates this parsimonious approach to blessings? One must be judicious about not reciting too many blessings because each includes an invocation of the name of God. Still, while the economical use of blessings may be a common theme in the materials, the unit does not work systematically through this problem. It touches on it from different angles probing the question from several sides. But in the final analysis this chapter does not thoroughly scrutinize a single unifying issue.

The applicable T.-passages pursue one of M.'s main concepts, enunciated earlier in the rules for Prayer. M. says, prayers replace Temple rituals. Hence regulations for Prayer are similar in some respects to the general principles of the rules for the cult. M. does not extend this analogy to food blessings. T. does, saying that one who does not recite the blessings over foods is like one who committed a sacrilege by eating Temple property (T. 4:1).

T. also develops a much more intricate and more highly specialized system of blessings than we find in M. (cf. T. 4:4-5 and esp. T. 5:15). This enterprise goes beyond just supplementing M. and develops new levels of specialization for food blessings. In independent supplements, T. distinguishes between raw, baked and cooked foods, and between loaves of bread and puddings (4:6-7). M. does not mention any of these distinctions.

T.'s remaining independent materials (e.g. 4:8) deal directly with the meal–regulations and customs for eating, washing and reclining at the formal dinner (cf. also T. 5:5-6). These rules reflect background materials which M. seems to take for granted that everyone knows (cf. M. 6:4-7).

Additional independent items refer to meal customs in Jerusalem (T. 4:9-11) and regulations for the interruption of daily meals (T. 4:19-21), of the Sabbath meal (T. 5:1-4). Other units deal with the notion of kingship in the tribes of Israel (4:18) and rules for etiquette during the meal (5:7-10). Miscellaneous rules close out the section (5:11-13).

6:1

A. What blessings do they recite over produce?

B. Over produce of the tree he says, "[Blessed art Thou, O Lord our God, King of the Universe,] creator of the fruit of the tree."

C. Except for wine, for over wine he says, "[Blessed art Thou, O Lord our God, King of the Universe] creator of the fruit of the vine.

D. Over vegetables [produce which grows in ground] he says, "[Blessed art Thou, O Lord our God, King of the Universe] creator of the fruit of the ground."

E. Except for bread, for over bread he says, "[Blessed art Thou, O Lord our God, King of the Universe] who brings forth bread from the earth."

F. And over [salad] greens he says, "Creator of the fruit of the ground."

G. R. Judah says, "Creator of diverse kinds of herbs."

As we have indicated, each blessing is a short formulaic sentence with a common invocation of God's name ("Blessed art Thou, O Lord, our God, King of the Universe") followed by a short specific phrase which mentions the type of food to be eaten. M.'s first premise is that before eating any food one must recite a blessing.

M. divides foods into two major categories, fruits and vegetables. Each group has its own specific blessing. Wine and bread have their own blessings since they are the primary staple foods of the diet (A-E). Judah considers salad greens to be a separate category—against the anonymous rule of M. (F-G).

6:2

A. If over the fruit of trees one [by error] recited the blessing, "Blessed [art Thou, O Lord our God, King of the Universe] creator of the fruit of the ground," he fulfilled his obligation [to recite a blessing over the food because trees do grow in the ground].

B. If over vegetables [one by error recited the blessing, "Blessed art Thou, O Lord our God, King of the Universe] creator of the fruit of the trees," he did not fulfill his obligation [because produce of the ground does not grow on trees].

C. If over any [fruits or vegetables] one [by error] recited, "For all came into being by his word," he fulfilled his obligation.

If one recites the wrong blessing, he has confused the categories and made an inappropriate statement and so does not fulfill his obligation. But M. adds a simple point. The blessings for vegetables is effective also for fruits. Both in reality grow in the ground. But the blessing for fruits does not serve for vegetables.

C introduces a third blessing formula, a catch-all for foods which do not fit the other categories, "For all came into being by his word."

6:3

A. Over something which does not grow in the earth, one says [the blessing], "For all came into being by his word."

B. Over vinegar, and over unripe fruit, and over edible locusts, one says [the blessing], "For all came into being by his word."

C. R. Judah says, "Over anything which is accursed [i.e. results from a destructive effort], one does not recite a blessing."

M. continues with further rulings for the foods subsumed by the general blessing, "For all came into being at his word." One recites this blessing over foods which do not grow in the ground (such as milk, cheese and eggs) or over edibles which are in some ways defective (vinegar, unripe fruit, locusts). Judah's gloss says it is not proper to invoke the name of God in a blessing over food which most people think of as a sign of a curse, e.g. soured, unripened food, or insects which strip the land of its bounty.

In all M. accepts five formulae of blessings: for fruit, for vegetables, for wine, for bread, for all other foods. It rejects one category of blessing: for herbs. How does one best apply these blessings in the complex context of a meal or dinner? That is the next subject to be addressed in our chapter.

T. 4:1

A. One may not taste anything until he recites a blessing [over it].

B. As it is written, "The earth and all therein is the Lord's" [Ps. 24:1].

C. One who derives any benefit from the world [by eating of its bounty] without first reciting a blessing, has committed a sacrilege.

D. [He may not derive any benefit] until [he fulfills all the obligations] which permit him [to derive benefit, i.e. recites the proper blessings].

E. One should make use of his face, his hands, and his feet only for the honor of his creator.

F. As Scripture states, "The Lord has made everything for its purpose" [Prov. 16:4, read as "Everything that God has made [should be used] for his sake, for his glory"].

In this autonomous supplement T. first justifies with a proof text from Scripture the rabbinic requirement of reciting a blessing before eating (A-B). The second part of the pericope, C-D makes an independent, but related comparison between the householder's use of ordinary food and a person's use of Temple sancta. This continues for the current topic, rules for food blessings, T.'s earlier development of the analogy between laws of prayer and rules for the Temple (e.g. T. 3:1). Here T. in effect says that the world is a Temple and only through the rabbinic rituals (e.g. blessings) may one use the Temple goods (e.g.

common foods). Although in the present context C-D refers to blessings for foods, this point may be extended to any action in which one benefits from the material goods of the world for which the rabbis require the recitation of a blessing (e.g. smelling spices, viewing natural wonders, etc.).

E-F completes the thought. All of one's actions, it says, should be for God's sake. One must conduct the common affairs of every-day life as a priest would conduct the affairs of the Temple cult, in sanctity. As usual T. phrases this consequential rabbinic statement in its characteristic compact and stylized rules.

T. 4:2

A. Date honey, apple cider, and vinegar made from late-ripening grapes–one recites a blessing over them just as one recites a blessing over fish sauce [fish brine mixed with wine and oil, even though the wine and oil in each mixture is no longer in its pure, best state].

T. seems to supplement M. 6:3. One recites the blessings, "For all came into being by his word," for fish brine, processed out of a derivative of fish, wine and oil. The same law applies to certain processed derivatives of dates, apples, or grapes. Lieberman's explanation (TK, p. 57) of this supplement is a bit homiletical. He artificially ties it to the preceding unit, T. 4:1. The point is that one still must recite a blessing before eating even derivative edibles, such as brine which derives its flavor from fish. Even though it is qualitatively less significant than the food they are derived from, these foods merit the same blessings.

T. 4:3

A. "Over wine in its natural state [undiluted] they recite, 'Blessed [art Thou, O Lord our God, King of the Universe] creator of the fruit of the tree.'
B. And they may wash their hands with it.
C. "Once the wine has been diluted, they say over it, 'Blessed [art Thou, O Lord our God, King of the Universe] creator of the fruit of the vine.'
D. And they may not wash their hands with it,"
E. the words of R. Eliezer.
F. And sages say, "Both over natural [wine] and over diluted [wine] they say, 'Blessed [art Thou, O Lord our God, King of the Universe] creator of the fruit of the vine.'
G. "And they may not wash their hands with it."

This T. supplements M. 6:1C. Eliezer in A-E considers unmixed wine to be a juice. It therefore requires the blessing of a juice and one may wash his hands in it. Once it is mixed with water it becomes wine, it has the blessing of wine, and it cannot be used for washing. Sages rule that unmixed grape juice has the same rule as mixed wine. Cf. also M. 7:5 for a simpler version of this dispute. Also note that it may have been a common ancient practice to wash one's hands with wine (see Petronius, Satyricon, 34, cited by Lieberman, TK, *ad. loc.*).

T. 4:4

A. If they brought before him types of desserts, he recites over them the blessing, "Creator of types of sweets."

B. Over edible seeds he recites, "Creator of types of seeds,"

C. and over other herbs he recites, "Creator of types of herbs."

D. And over greens he recites, "Creator of the fruit of the ground" [M. Ber. 6:1F].

E. R. Judah says, "[He recites, 'Blessed [art Thou, O Lord], who at his word causes the ground to sprout.'"

F. R. Meir says, "Even if one saw a loaf [of bread] and said, 'Blessed be He who created this object. How beautiful it is,' he fulfilled his obligation."

T. 4:5

G. [Or] "if one saw figs and said, 'Blessed be He who created these figs, how nice they are,' that serves as their blessing."

H. R. Yose says, "Anyone who departs from the formula which the sages established for blessings has not fulfilled his obligation."

I. R. Judah says, "[If one eats] any food which was changed from its natural state [by processing], and departed [on that account] from the [established] benedictory formula–he has fulfilled his obligation."

T.'s supplements demonstrate that its system of food blessings is more complex than M.'s. M. listed only five categories of blessings: for fruit of the ground, of the tree, of the vine, bread, and a general blessing. T. has special blessings for desserts (A), seeds (B), and herbs (C). D-E gives an alternative version of Judah's gloss to M. 6:1.

T. 4:4F, continued at 4:5A, then provides us with Meir's rule allowing variation in the formula of a blessing. If one recites a formula of praise over the beauty of bread or figs, that may serve in place of its standard blessing.

Yose's rule conflicts with Meir's, though not in a direct dispute. The law is independent of the preceding. The last two rules, Yose vs. Judah, are formally one unit. According to Yose no one has the authority to change the formula of a rabbinic blessing. Judah qualifies this with a further rule. One may alter the formula of the blessing for a processed food.

T. significantly expands M. 6:1's simple system of blessings both here and in the materials which follow. Later in this chapter T. also appends a large amount of material about the dinner and regulations for its procedures.

T. 4:6

A. He who chews grains of wheat, recites over them [the blessing], "Creator of types of seeds."

B. If one baked or cooked [a dish using pieces of wheat bread in his recipe]–

C. as long as the pieces remain intact, he must recite over [the dish] before eating, "He who brings forth bread from the earth,"

D. and he must recite over it three blessing [i.e. grace] after eating. [It has the same requirements as the bread itself.]

E. If the pieces do not remain intact [in the dish] he must recite over it [before eating], "Creator of types of grains,"

F. and must recite over it after eating one blessing which is an abstract of the three blessings.

T. 4:7

A. He who chews grains of rice, recites over them the blessing, "Creator of the fruit of the ground."

B. If one baked or cooked [a dish using pieces of rice loaves in his recipe],

C. even if the pieces remain intact he recites over [the dish] before eating, "Creator of types of grains"

D. and he need not recite a blessing over it after eating. [It has the same requirements as the rice loaves themselves.]

E. This is the general rule:

F. All [those foods over which] one recites over them before eating, "He who brings forth bread from the earth"

G. after eating one recites [over them] three blessings [i.e. grace after meals].

In this independent unit T. expands further on its additional categories of blessings presented first at T. 4:4A-C. It is based on the rules for blessings set out in T. 4:4 and on the concern of T. 4:5 with processed foods. T. (A) treats raw wheat as a seed. Hence its blessing is, "Creator of types of seeds."

The unit's second issue is the proper sequence of blessings for eating a pudding made out of wheat bread (B-F). Before eating it one recites the blessing for bread, if pieces of bread are still visible. And one recites the three meal blessings after eating, as if he had eaten bread. If the pieces of bread are not identifiable, one recites a more general blessing, "Creator of types of grains," and afterward he recites one blessing as if he had eaten only grains or cereal. All this is fairly straightforward.

Next T. 4:7 turns to the more complex issue of the blessings recited over rice and rice pudding. T. first treats rice as if it were a vegetable not a grain. The blessing for eating grains of rice then is, "Creator of the fruit of the ground," as for vegetables (A). But then T. considers rice pudding, for the purposes of reciting a blessing, to be equivalent to cakes made of grain. That means that the blessing one recites for rice pudding is, "Creator of types of grains" (B-C). After eating the pudding one need not recite any blessing, the same as the rule for rice cakes themselves. Rice then has a dual identity. On the one hand, eaten alone it requires the blessing of a vegetable. On the other hand, eaten as part of a pudding it requires the blessing of a grain.

To review, T. distinguishes among raw, baked, and cooked foods, and between loaves of bread and pudding. M. makes no mention of any of these distinctions.

Finally, T. 4:7E-G translates the specific case of T. 4:6C-D into a general rule. For bread and breadstuffs for which before eating one recites the blessing for bread, such as the bread pudding of the preceding unit, after eating it one recites the three meal blessings.

To sum up, T. adds to M.'s system of five basic categories of blessings recited before eating foods, two others: one for seeds, and one for grains. T. also differentiates between several kinds of prepared foods, as we explained.

T.'s next unit leaves the subject of the categories of food blessings and turns to several pericopae which supplement M. and provide some background that M. chapter six takes for granted, assorted regulations and customs for the dinner.

6:4

A. If one had before him many kinds [of food]–

B. R. Judah says, "If among them there is a food of the seven kinds [of foods of the Land of Israel], one must recite the blessing over that [food first]."

C. And sages say, "[One may recite the blessing] over any [food] he wishes."

M. assumes that when one eats several different foods at the same time he needs to recite only one blessing. The question then is which blessing, over which food, takes priority? Judah stipulates that foods which are of the seven kinds of food of the Land of Israel take priority over other foods. This refers to the foods mentioned in Deut. 8:8: "A land of wheat and barley, of vines and fig trees and pomegranates, a land of olive trees and honey." Sages rely on a more subjective criterion. One recites a blessing over whichever food he prefers.

6:5

A. If one recited the blessing over wine [which he drank] before the meal, he exempted [himself from the obligation to recite a blessing over] the wine [which he drinks] after the meal.

B. If one recited the blessing over an appetizer [which he ate] before the meal, he exempted [himself from the obligation to recite a blessing over] the appetizer [which he eats] after the meal.

C. If one recited the blessing over bread, he exempted [himself from the obligation to recite the blessing over] the appetizer.

D. If one recited the blessing over the appetizer, he did not exempt [himself from the obligation to recite a blessing over] the bread.

E. The House of Shammai say, [By reciting a blessing over the appetizer one does] not even [exempt himself from his obligation to recite a blessing over] a potted dish."

M.'s rule relates to the context of a structured dinner during which the participants may first drink wine and eat appetizers, then have a meal, then again drink wine and eat appetizers. One blessing suffices for the wine one drinks both before and after the meal, M. says. And one blessing is enough for the appetizers one eats before and after the meal (A-B). Again, as above in 6:4, M. assumes that one must be economical in his use of blessings.

C-E deals with a related subject. During the meal, once one has recited the blessing over bread, he need not recite the blessing over an appetizer. But one who recites a blessings over an appetizer, must still recite the blessing over bread. This ruling adumbrates the principle of 6:7B below. One recites a blessings over a primary food and thereby exempts himself from the requirement to recite a blessing over a secondary food. The redactor adds the House of Shammai's gloss to support the rule of D. But it does not fit integrally into the construction of the pericope. It dangles at the end of this unit, apparently appended as an afterthought.

6:6

A. When they are sitting [prior to a meal], each person recites the blessings for himself.

B. When they recline [on couches at the meal together], one person recites the blessings for all of them.

C. When they bring out wine during the meal, each person recites the blessings for himself [because they drink by themselves].

D. [When they bring out wine] after the meal, one person recites the blessings for all of them [because they drink together].

E. And [that person] says the blessing over the incense, even though they bring out the incense only after dinner [when they already may be sitting by themselves].

As in the preceding unit, this pericope's rules relate to the context of the formal dinner. This section adds to our rules for the rabbinic archetypical conception of the dinner. Its stages are: preceding the meal the participants sit together on chairs or benches, drink wine and eat appetizers and wait as all the guests assemble. The meal itself follows. After the meal is cleared away, the guests remain, again drink wine and eat appetizers and they may also burn incense.

M.'s question is must each individual recite a blessing over the food he eats? For food prior to the meal, an appetizer, each recites his own blessing. They recite blessings as individuals. For food during the meal, one person recites a blessing for all those who eat together (A-B). When they eat the meal they become a unified collective fellowship. The procedure for wine differs. Each individual recites the blessing over the wine he drinks during the meal. But after the meal one person may recite a blessing for all those who drink wine together. During the meal they eat as a collective. After the meal they drink together.

Finally, even though they may burn incense after they complete the formal structure of the dinner, one person may recite the blessing over the fragrance of the incense on behalf of all those assembled because they benefit collectively from its aroma.

T. 4:8

A. What is the order of the dinner?

B. When the guests enter, they sit on benches or on chairs while all [the guests] assemble.

C. Once they all have assembled, and they bring out [water for washing] their hands,

D. each person washes one hand [so that he may hold in it the cup of wine.]

E. When [they bring out and] mix the wine, each person recites the blessing for himself.

F. When they bring out appetizers each person recites the blessing for himself.

G. When they get up [from the chairs] and recline [on couches to eat the rest of the meal], and they bring out [water for washing] their hands,

H. even though they each had already washed one hand they now must wash both hands [to eat].

I. When they [bring out and] mix the wine, even though they recited a blessing over the first cup, they now recite a blessing over the second cup. [And one person recites the blessing for all of them.]

J. When they bring out an appetizer, [even though they recited a blessing over the first, they now recite a blessing over the second].

K. And one person recites the blessing for all of them.

L. A guest may not enter [to join the meal] if he comes after three appetizers are served.

In this independent unit T. spells out some procedures for the dinner and the meal as background for M.'s rules. The dinner, as T. more fully describes it, is a highly formalized occasion of table fellowship. B-F describes the preliminary dinner customs for before the meal. As the participants gather together they sit, wash, recite blessings, drink wine and eat appetizers. These are the wine and appetizers which they eat before the meal mentioned in M. 6:5A. T. rules that each recites his own blessing for the wine and appetizer which he eats before the meal (E-F). This corresponds with M. 6:6A which refers to the practice of each person reciting his own blessing on food that he eats before the meal.

G-K deal with the meal itself. The participants must wash again, recite the blessing over the wine again, and over the appetizer again. This reflects the implied rule of M. 6:5A-B. According to M. one who recited a blessing over the wine or appetizer before the meal exempted himself from the obligation to recite a blessing over the same items eaten after the meal. The implication is that one still must recite the blessing over these items eaten in the meal itself, as T.'s present ruling tells us.

T. 4:8I is ambiguous concerning the procedure for reciting blessings over the wine during the meal. It says nothing about who recites. But as we have interpolated, it is reasonable to assume that one person may recite the blessing for all others over the wine they drink during the meal. This rule is not quite so obvious since M. 6:6C specifically makes the point that unlike the procedure for appetizers, each recites his own blessing over the wine they drink at the meal. If T.'s rules correspond to M.'s, we must assume that during the meal each recites his own blessing over wine.

T. further specifies that one person may recite the blessing over the appetizer on behalf of all those assembled (K). This agrees with the ruling of M. 6:6B, which says that one person recites the blessings for all those assembled at the meal.

As is evident, T. takes up its own interests, and systematically presents its materials in this neatly arranged unit. T. focuses in this pericope on the dinner itself and its procedures rather than on M.'s main topic, the economical use of blessings over food. This difference in perspective is readily evident in the unit, as it shares many of M.'s assumptions, as shown, but diverges in its focus and structure.

T.'s last line here reports on a custom of dinner etiquette. One who comes late to join the gathering is not permitted to enter if three appetizers have already been served. T. continues to present further customs for the dinner in the next few pericopae.

T. 4:9

A. Said R. Simeon b. Gamaliel, "This was a noteworthy custom in Jerusalem:

B. "They spread open a cloth in the doorway.

C. "As long as the cloth is spread out, guests may enter.

D. "Once the cloth has been closed, guests are not allowed to enter."

T. 4:10

A. And there was another custom in Jerusalem:

B. they cede [responsibility for the preparation and serving of] the meal to the chef.

C. If anything goes amiss during the meal, they punish the chef.

D. [The degree of the punishment] all depends on the honor due the guests and on the honor due the host.

T. 4:11

A. A ruling regarding the communal meal:

B. one who leaves to urinate must wash one hand [upon returning].

C. [One who goes out] to speak to his fellow and walked a distance must wash both his hands [upon returning].

D. Where does he wash?

E. He enters and sits in his place and washes.

F. And the jug of water is passed among all the guests.

This unit continues the preceding independent supplements to M. Simeon's rule in T. 4:9 presents an alternative to the anonymous law of 4:8L. The custom in Jerusalem is once they draw the curtain at the collective dinner new guests may not enter to join the assembly.

Two further miscellaneous laws about the dinner follow. A second Jerusalem custom is for the chef to take responsibility if anything goes amiss in the dinner (T. 4:10). Another item states that one who leaves the group during the dinner to attend to his needs must wash at the table when he returns (T. 4:11).

T. 4:12

A. They asked Ben Zoma, "Why does it say, *When they bring out wine during the meal, each person recites the blessing for himself* [M. 6:6C]?"

B. He said to them, "It is because [while one eats] his throat is not clear. [He may choke if he speaks to respond 'Amen' to the leader's blessing]."

T. cites and comments directly on M. providing for us a simple reason for Ben Zoma's ruling that each recites his own blessing for wine which they drink during the meal.

6:7

A. When they bring out for him first a salted relish, and with it bread, he recites the blessing over the salted relish, and exempts [himself from the requirement of reciting a blessing over] the bread, for [in such a case] the bread is secondary to it.

B. This is the general rule: Over any primary food which is accompanied by a secondary food, one recites the blessing over the primary food and exempts [himself thereby from reciting the blessing over the] secondary food.

During the meal when one eats a dish with bread, and the dish is primary, the bread is secondary. He recites the blessing over the dish, not over the bread (A). Based on M. 6:5C-D we would have thought the contrary, that a blessing for an appetizer does not suffice for bread. But in this present case the appetizer, the salted relish, serves as the main dish of the meal. Since it is the primary food, its blessing takes precedence. B's general rule sums up the matter.

M.'s interest in blessings recited before eating ends with this rule. Next it turns briefly to regulations for blessings which follow the meal.

T. 4:13

A. [If] they brought before him [cf. M. Ber. 6:7] rice and wine, he recites a blessing over the rice and exempts [thereby] the wine [from the need for a separate blessing];

B. [if they brought before him] radishes and unripe fruit–he recites a blessing over the radishes and exempts [thereby] the unripe fruit [from the need for a separate blessing].

T. 4:14

A. [If they brought before him] salted relish and a piece [of bread]–he recites a blessing over the salted relish and exempts [thereby] the piece [of bread] [from the need for a separate blessing; cf. M. Ber. 6:7].

B. R. Haninah b. Gamaliel says, "[Both] the salted relish [E: the loaf] which is brought out at the outset before the [main] meal and the loaf which is brought out with the salted relish after the meal require a blessing before and after [eating] them."

C. R. Simeon b. Gamaliel says, "Pieces [of bread] serve as an important sign for the guests.

D. "Whenever the guests see the pieces [being brought out], they know that something else [viz., some other course] is to follow them.

E. "[If they see] a whole loaf [or] fish and beans [being served], they know that nothing else is to follow them."

The point of M. 6:7 is that the blessing which one recites over a primary food exempts him from reciting another blessing over a secondary food. This rule applies even where the primary food is ordinarily considered lower in priority than the secondary food.

T. 4:13 adds two further illustrations of M.'s general rule. Where one eats rice and wine, one recites the blessing over the rice which is primary. One need not recite the blessing over the wine (A). Without this rule one might have thought that for blessings, wine is primary and that the secondary grain, rice, is of lower priority.

When confronted with a choice between an unimportant vegetable and an unripe fruit, B tells us that one recites the blessing over the vegetable. It takes priority over unformed fruits.

4:14 A repeats M. 6:6A with a small modification. M.'s law applies only to a piece of bread, not to a whole loaf. T.'s bases its on the rule which follows at B. There Haninah says that if one has a relish and a loaf he must recite the blessings before and after the loaf, as if it were a separate meal in itself.

C-E add miscellaneous rules to A-B, providing further remarks about the place of pieces of bread and whole loaves in the meal.

6:8

A. "If one ate figs, or grapes, or pomegranates [as the main dish of his meal], he recites over them [after eating them the grace after meals comprised of] three blessings," the words of R. Gamaliel.

B. And sages say, "[He recites] one blessing [which embodies the substance of the full grace after meals]."

C. R. Aqiba says, "Even if one ate cooked vegetables, and that was [the main dish of] his meal, [after eating them] he recites over them three blessings."

D. One who drinks water to quench his thirst says, "Blessed [art Thou, O Lord our God, King of the Universe,] for all came into being by his word."

E. R. Tarfon says, "He says, ['Blessed art Thou, O Lord our God, King of the Universe,] Creator of many souls and their needs."

M. deals with the blessings one recites after the meal. If one ate bread as a full main course, after eating he must recite the complete grace, the three blessings. The dispute at A-B relates to one who ate only fruit as a meal. Gamaliel says that also may constitute a full meal and require the recitation of the entire grace after meals, the three blessings.

Sages say no. One recites a shorter liturgy, one blessing which embodies the three meal blessings. Aqiba's ruling goes furthest. He requires that one who ate vegetables as the main course of his meal also must recite the full three blessings after eating. For Aqiba, a person's intent is the most important factor. Regardless of how a food is classified objectively, if one considers it the main part of his meal, he must recite over it after eating the appropriate formal grace of three blessings.

D-E concludes the chapter with the rules for the blessings recited upon drinking water. Before drinking one recites, "For all" (D). After drinking he recites the short blessing which concludes, "Creator of many souls" (E).

T. 4:15

A. [When a person has before him several foods to eat at a meal—] he recites the blessing over the breadstuff which is of the highest quality.

B. How so?

C. [If one has before him] a [whole] fine loaf and a whole home-made loaf [of the same grain],

D. he says [the blessing] over the whole fine loaf.

E. [If one has] a piece of a fine loaf and a whole home-made loaf,

F. he says [the blessing] over the whole home-made loaf.

G. [If one has] wheat bread and barley bread,

H. he says [the blessing] over the wheat bread.

I. [If one has] a piece of wheat bread and a whole barley bread,

J. he says [the blessing] over the piece of wheat bread.

K. [If one has] a barley bread and a spelt bread,

L. one says [the blessing] over the barley bread.

M. But is not spelt bread better [quality] than barley bread?

N. But barley is one of the seven kinds [of produce of the Land of Israel, mentioned in Deut. 8:8] and spelt is not one of the seven kinds.

O. This is the general rule:

P. Concerning any food that is made from produce of one of the seven kinds or of a kind of breadstuff,

Q. Rabban Gamaliel says, "One recites three blessings [of the Grace after meals] after [eating] it,

R. And sages say, "[He recites] one blessing [the abbreviated grace]."

S. One time Rabban Gamaliel and the elders were seated at a table in Jericho.

T. They [attendants] brought before them dates [after they had finished the meal] and they ate them.

U. R. Aqiba precipitously recited one [blessing] after [eating] them.

V. Said to him Rabban Gamaliel, "Aqiba, why do you poke your head into disputes?"

W. He [Aqiba] said to him, "Did you not teach us 'One should follow the majority'? [cf. Exod. 23:2]"

X. "Even though you rule one way and your fellows rule another way, the halakhah follows the ruling of the majority."

Y. R. Judah says in his [Gamaliel's] name, "All [dishes] that are made from the seven kinds [of produce of the Land of Israel], but not of kinds of breadstuff,

Z. or made of kinds of breadstuff, but not baked into a loaf,

AA. R. Gamaliel says, 'One recites three blessings after eating it.'

BB. And sages say, '[He recites] one blessing.'

CC. "And all dishes which are made neither from the seven kinds, nor from kinds of breadstuff,

DD. R. Gamaliel says, 'One recites [before and] after it [one blessing].'

EE. And sages say, '[One recites a blessing before eating, and one recites after it] nothing.'"

This long and complex pericope is in two major parts. The first independent section bears some relation to the issue raised in M. 6:4 above. A-N establishes a hierarchy of priorities for breads and bread products. The general principles are that fine baker's loaves are superior to home-made loaves. Whole loaves are above broken loaves. Wheat bread is superior to barley bread and barley bread to spelt bread.

T. spells out some of the more complex distinctions within these given parameters. A whole home-made bread takes precedence over a broken fine bread (E-F). A broken wheat loaf is superior to a whole barley loaf (I-J).

Finally M-N reflects Judah's rule in M. 6:4B. Where all other conditions are equal, a bread made from one of the grains mentioned in Scripture takes precedence over a bread made from another variety of grain.

O-R opens the second section of this pericope with a dispute over the blessings after eating, an alternative version of the dispute at M. 6:8A-B. The mention of breadstuffs in the protasis of this dispute may account for the long preceding excursus on the subject of priorities in types of breads and bread products. In the story which follows (S-X) Aqiba supports the view of sages against Gamaliel. As Lieberman points out (TK, *ad. loc.*), Aqiba's view here is not necessarily inconsistent with his ruling in Mishnah. Here we speak of a case in which one ate dates after his meal. In M. 6:8C Aqiba's main point was that one must recite three blessings after anything one eats for the main course of his meal.

Last, T. adds in Judah's name yet another version of the dispute, essentially the same as the preceding (Y-EE). At CC-EE Judah extends the dispute to the question of the blessing one recites after eating foods which are neither of the seven kinds nor of breadstuff. In that case, Judah tells us, Gamaliel will rule that one recites one blessing after eating. Sages will say that one does not need to recite any blessing after eating such foods.

T. 4:16

A. Once R. Tarfon was sitting in the shade of a dovecote on a Sabbath afternoon.

B. They [attendants] brought before him a pail of cool water.

C. He said to his students, "One who drinks water to quench his thirst—what blessing does he recite?"

D. They said to him, "Teach us, our master."

E. He said to them, "[Blessed art Thou, O Lord,] Creator of creatures and their needs."

F. He said to them, "May I inquire [into the meaning of Scripture]?"

G. They said to him, "Teach us, our master."

H. He said to them, "Behold Scripture states, 'Then they [Joseph's brothers] sat to eat; and looking up they saw [a caravan of Ishmaelites coming from Gilead, with their camels bearing gum, balm, and myrrh, on their way to carry it down to Egypt]' (Gen. 37:25). Now it is customary for Arabs to carry only foul-smelling skins with resin.

I. "But [God saw to it that] they put that righteous man [Joseph] among [sweet-smelling and] desirable things.

J. "And may we not reason *a fortiori:* if, when God is angry at the righteous, he has mercy on them, when he is disposed to be merciful, how much more so [does he have mercy on them]!

T. 4:17

A. "Similarly, 'They drew near and they carried them' [the corpses of Nadab and Abihu] 'in their coats out of the camp' (Lev. 10:5).

B. "And may we not reason *a fortiori:* if, when God is angry at the righteous, [their treatment is] such, when he is disposed to be merciful, how much more so [is he mindful of their honor]!

C. "Similarly, 'The lion had not eaten the body [of the disobedient man of God from Judah] or torn the ass' (I Kings 13:28).

D. "And may we not reason *a fortiori:* if, when God is angry at the righteous, and he has mercy on them, when he is disposed to be merciful, how much more so [does he have mercy on them]!"

E. He [Tarfon] said, "May I inquire [into the meaning of Scripture]?"

F. They [his students] said to him, "Teach us, our master."

G. He said to them, "Why did Judah merit [that] the kingship [be assigned by God to his tribe]?"

H. [Lieberman supplies: They said to him,] "Because he confessed [in the incident] concerning Tamar" [cf. Gen. 34:26].

T. 4:18

A. Once Four elders were sitting in the gate house of R. Joshua: Eleazar b. Matiah, Hananiah b. Kinai, Simeon b. Azzai, and Simeon the Yemenite,

B. and they were busy studying that which Aqiba [ed. princ.: Tarfon] had taught them [ed. princ. adds: Said to them R. Aqiba]:

C. "Why did Judah merit [that] the kingship [be assigned to his tribe]?"

D. "Because he confessed [in the incident] concerning Tamar."

E. They themselves added [to the teaching]: "What wise men have told, and their fathers have not hidden, to whom alone the land was given [and no stranger passed among them] (Job 15:18-19)."

F. He [Tarfon] said to them, "And do we reward [people] for [their] transgressions?

G. "Why, then, did Judah merit the kingship?"

H. [They replied,] "Because he saved his brother [Joseph] from death,

I. "as Scripture states, 'Then Judah said to his brothers, What profit [is it if we slay our brother and conceal his blood]? (Gen. 37:26).

J. He said to them, "It is sufficient that the rescue atoned for the sale [of their brother into slavery, but it does not merit a reward].

K. "Why, then, did Judah merit the kingship?"

L. They said to him, "Because of his humility,

M. "as Scripture states, 'Now therefore, let your servant, I pray you, remain instead of the lad [as a slave to my lord; and let the lad go back with his brothers'] (Gen. 44:33).

N. "Saul, too, merited the kingship only because of his humility,

O. "as Scripture states, '[Saul said to his servant who was with him,] 'Come, let us go back lest my father cease to care about the asses and become anxious about us" (I Sam. 9:5).

P. "He valued his servant equally with himself.

Q. "But Samuel did not speak this way. Rather, [he said], 'Your father has ceased to care about the asses and is anxious about you, saying, 'What shall I do about my son?" (I Sam. 10:2).

R. "[So, too,] when he [Saul] flees from [the mantle of] rulership what does Scripture state?

S. "'So they inquired again of the Lord, 'Did the man come hither?' and the Lord said, 'Behold, he has hidden himself among the baggage" (I Sam. 10:22)."

T. He [Tarfon] said to them, "But he [Judah] served as a suretor [for Joseph], and a suretor ultimately is freed from his surety [so there is no great merit in this action].

U. "Why, then, did Judah merit the kingship?"

V. They said to him, "Teach us, our master."

W. He said to them, "Because he sanctified the name of the Holy One, blessed be He, at the sea.

X. "When the tribes came and stood at the sea, this one said, 'I shall descend [first into the sea]' and this one said, 'I shall descend [first into the sea].' The tribe of Judah took the initiative [lit., jumped] and descended first [into the sea] and [thereby] sanctified the name of God at the sea.

Y. "And concerning that hour Scripture states, 'Save me, O God! For the waters have come up to my neck. I sink in deep mire, where there is no foothold' (Ps. 69:2-3 [= RSV 69:1-2])... 'Let not the flood sweep over me' (ibid. 16 [- RSV 15]...And Scripture states, 'Judah became his sanctuary [קדשו: his sanctified; read: his 'sanctifier'] (Ps. 114:2). Judah sanctified the name of God at the sea. Therefore, 'Israel [is] his dominion' (ibid.)."

This lengthy unit begins with a reference to the last concern of our M., the blessing one recites over the drinking water (A-E). The remainder of the unit takes up the subject of the rewards that the saints of Israel will receive. 4:18 deals with the explanations of why God assigned kingship to the tribe of Judah as a reward. Judah did not merit the reward of kingship for his tribe because he confessed his sins (C-E), or because he worked out a compromise to save a life (H-J), or because of his humility (K-T), but rather because his tribe was the first to face the mortal danger of potential martyrdom at the sea (U-Y). This lengthy teaching with messianic overtones glorifies activist attitudes even at the risk of martyrdom.

T. 4:19

A. [If] they left [the communal meal in order] to escort the bride [to the meal, as long as] they have left behind even an old or sickly man,

B. they need not recite the blessing [after meals] over [the food] which they had eaten prior [to leaving],

C. and when they resume [the meal], they need not recite a blessing as [would be done] at the beginning [of a new meal].

D. [If] they did not leave behind an old or sickly man,

E. they must recite the blessing [after meals] over [the food] which they had eaten prior [to leaving],

F. and when they resume [the meal], they must recite a blessing as [would be done] at the beginning [of a new meal].

T. 4:20

A. A householder who was reclining at table and eating—

B. [if] his friend called him [away from the table] to speak with him,

C. he need not [first] recite the blessing [after meals] over [the food] which he had eaten prior [to leaving the table], and when he resumes [this meal], he need not recite a blessing as [would be done] at the beginning [of a new meal].

D. [If] he walked a distance [from where he had been eating, or interrupted his meal for a long period to time],

E. he must recite the blessing [after meals] over [the food] which he had eaten prior [to the interruption], and when he resumes [his meal], he must recite a blessing as [would be done] at the beginning [of a new meal].

T. 4:21

A. Workers who were picking figs, or harvesting dates, or harvesting olives,

B. even though they stop and eat from time to time,

C. need not recite the blessing [after meals] over [the food] which they had eaten prior [to the interruption], and when they resume [eating], they need not recite a blessing as would be done at the beginning [of a new meal].

D. If they walked a distance [from their work or interrupted it for a long period of time], they must recite the blessing [after meals] over [the food] which they had eaten prior [to the interruption], and when they resume [eating], they must recite a blessing as would be done at the beginning [of a new meal].

T. turns to entirely independent concerns for the remainder of this chapter and the beginning of the next. Earlier at 4:9-11 T. presented some independent rules for mealtime practice. It dealt there with entry into and interruption of the meal. Here it continues with materials dealing with customs for the meal. 4:19-21 take up other cases of interruptions of the meal.

4:19 says that if the entire party leaves to go and join a wedding celebration they need not start the dinner over again when they return as long as they leave behind at least one person to insure the continuity of the meal.

4:20 continues on the subject of interruption of the meal. One who goes out of the dining place for a casual conversation (A-C) need not begin the meal ritual anew when he returns. But if he goes away from the place (D-E) he must end the prior meal with the appropriate blessings for the meal, and begin again with an appropriate blessing before eating the food when he returns.

4:21 deals with yet another kind of interruption. Even though a worker may eat intermittently during the harvest he need not recite a new blessing each time he eats unless he leaves off from his work.

To review, T. deals in this section with three different cases of interruptions: where most of the participants interrupt the meal (4:19); where one person leaves the meal (4:20); and where one person eats on and off during his work in the harvest (4:21).

T. 5:1

A. "A man should not eat on the eve of the Sabbath from afternoon onwards,

B. "so that he should be hungry at the start of the Sabbath," the words of R. Judah.

C. R. Yose says, "He may continue to eat until it grows dark."

T. 5:2

A. Once Rabban Simeon b. Gamaliel and R. Judah and R. Yose were reclining [and eating] in Acre and the Sabbath began.

B. Said Rabban Simeon b. Gamaliel to R. Yose, "Rabbi, if it is your wish, we shall stop [eating] on account of the [beginning of the] Sabbath."

C. He said to him, "Every day you prefer my opinion to Judah's, and now you prefer Judah's opinion to mine!?

D. "[This verse expresses my reaction,] 'Will you also assault the queen in my presence, in my own house' (Esther 7:8)?"

E. He said to him, "If so, then let us not stop, lest the law be established permanently [in accord with our actions]."

F. They said [concerning this incident], "They did not move from there before the law was established according to R. Yose's [opinion]."

T. 5:3

A. Guests who were sitting [and eating] with a householder when the Sabbath began,

B. and they [the guests] got up at nightfall and went to the house of study and returned, and then the cup [of wine] was mixed for them—

C. "they recite over it [i.e., the cup] the [blessing about the] sanctification of the day," the words of R. Judah.

D. R. Yose says, "They may continue to eat until it grows dark."

T. 5:4

A. [When] they have mixed for him the first cup [of wine], he recites over it the blessing for the meal,

B. [and] mentions the Sabbath in the blessing for the meal,

C. and over the second [cup] he recites the sanctification of the day.

This group of traditions relates to the preceding only because it initially appears to be interested in whether one must interrupt a meal on Friday. More precisely its issue is whether a person must refrain from eating a meal on Friday afternoon so that he is hungry at the start of the Sabbath on Friday evening.

5:1 is a juxtaposition of different opinions, not a real dispute. The issue in common to both Judah and Yose is whether one may eat on Friday afternoon. Judah says that one should not eat at all. Yosah's (Yose's) view is that they need not refrain from eating. This same lemma, attributed to Yose, is attached again in a second context immediately below at 5:3. The story at 5:2 obviously supports Yose's view.

T. 5:5

A. What is the order for reclining [when several eat together]? [cf. T. Ber. 4:8, M. Ber. 6:6]

B. When there are two couches,

C. the greatest [in importance] among them reclines at the head of the first,

D. the second [in importance] to him reclines below him [at his feet].

E. When there are three couches,

F. the greatest [in importance] reclines at the head of the middle [couch],

G. the second [in importance] to him [reclines] above him, the third [in importance] below him.

H. In this manner they would go on and arrange [the rest of the guests in order].

T. 5:6

A. What is the order for washing hands?

B. For [a group of] up to five people–

C. they start [washing] with the highest in rank [i.e. most important person].

D. For more than this–they start [washing] with the lowest in rank [so the important people do not have to wait for long between washing and the meal]. [*Editio princeps* adds here: (And they proceed) until they reach the fifth (person), then they begin again with the greatest. And (the person who is seated) at the place where the water (for washing hands) after (the meal) comes back (after circulating around the table) recites the blessing (i.e., the one who washes last after the meal has the honor of reciting the blessing)].

E. What is the order for mixing the cup?

F. In the middle of the meal they start [to mix the cup] from the highest [in rank].

G. At the end of the meal, they start from the one who recites the blessing [i.e. the blessings over the meal].

H. If he [who is going to recite the blessings over the meal] wished to honor his master or someone who is more important than himself [by letting him receive the first cup of wine], he may do so.

These two units continue T. 4:8's description of the order of practices at the fellowship dinner.

T. 5:7

A. Two wait for another [to begin eating] with regard to [partaking food from] a single plate.

B. Three do not wait.

C. The one who recites the blessing [before eating] stretches forth his hand first [to partake of the food].

D. But if he wished to give the honor [of partaking first] to his master or to one who is greater than he in [mastery of] Torah, he may do so.

T. 5:8

A. One should not take a bite from a piece [of bread] and return it to the [common] plate, on account of mortal danger [to others who may thereby be infected by communicable diseases].

T. 5:9

A. One should not drink from a cup and then give it to his fellow, since people's constitutions are not always the same.

T. 5:10

A. One who serves [a meal to] two [others] may eat with them [in order to form the requisite quorum of three men for extending the invitation to recite grace after meals; cf. M. Ber. 7:1].

B. [If he serves a meal to] three [others], he may not eat with them,

C. unless they give him permission.

5:7 supplements 5:6 with two rules. A triplicate on practices of etiquette at the meal follows at 5:8-10.

T. 5:11

A. [If] a sweet morsel was brought to them during the meal,

B. one recites a blessing over the meal and [thereby] exempts the sweet morsel [from the necessity of a separate blessing].

T. 5:12

A. R. Muna says in the name of R. Judah [who said in the name of R. Yose the Galilean], 'Over a dessert cake [which one eats] after the meal, one is required to recite blessings before and after [eating it].'"

T. 5:13

A. [Washing one's hands with] water before the meal is optional. [Washing one's hands with] water after the meal is compulsory.

B. But with regard to the first case [i.e. before the meal] one washes and waits.

C. And with regard to the second case [i.e. after the meal] one washes and does not wait.

Three miscellanies close this lengthy Toseftan segment. 5:11-12 deal with blessings over desserts and return us to the subject of M. 6:8, blessings after eating. 5:13 appears to further supplement T. 5:6 or T. 4:8.

Chapter Seven

Berakhot Chapter Seven
The Invitation to Recite the Blessings after the Meal

At 6:8 above, M. deals briefly with the blessings one recites after eating. In this chapter M. focuses on rules for forming a quorum for the recitation of the blessings after the meal. M. assumes that three or more persons who eat a meal together must recite the meal blessings together as a collective fellowship. This process is called "זימון," inviting, because one member of the group is appointed to call together to recite the blessings all those who participated in the meal. Here we focus on the rules for the call by the leader at the meal to the others assembled there to recite the blessings (grace) after the meal.

M. spells out with some care the procedures for extending the invitation for reciting the grace after meals. First it enunciates the general assumption that a minimum of three who ate a meal together constitute a quorum and must appoint a leader and recite the meal blessings as a fellowship (7:1A). Next M. lists those categories of people who may be counted for the quorum, and those who may not be included. Whether or not one may be included depends on what kind of food and how much food the person ate and on the class or status of the individual (M. 7:1B-7:2D).

M. next turns to the formula the leader recites to call the group together for the meal blessings (7:3). In accord with a ruling attributed to Yose the Galilean, this formula varies according to the size of the assembled fellowship. Other traditions ascribed to Aqiba and Ishmael in a dispute are appended here and limit this rule.

The remaining units address the issue of how and under what circumstances a single group may separate to recite the meal blessings (7:4) or separate groups may join together to form a quorum to appoint someone to extend the invitation to recite the blessings for the meal (7:5A-B). A miscellaneous rule about the kind of wine over which one may recite a blessing concludes the chapter and serves as a transition to the concerns of the next unit.

Unfortunately, there is no direct evidence of the earliest development or the provenance of the practices discussed in the present chapter. Except for the gloss of Judah (7:2D) and for the Yavnean materials (7:3I-K), the chapter is made up of anonymous materials.

The Yavnean traditions in 7:2 do not help us date the origin of these laws. These traditions make sense both in the present context and independent of this setting, perhaps as laws which regulate the recitation of the blessings of the Prayer service. It is therefore possible that when our redactor located these lemmas here he imposed on the rulings his own interpretation that they were relevant to the present issues. We can say only that by the time of the generation of the redaction of M. these rules for the invitation to recite the blessings of the meal were known and circulated. From the present traditions we cannot infer much more about the development of this fellowship practice.

T.'s pertinent concerns here relate to M. but stand independent of M.'s immediate concerns. T. is interested in whether recitation of the blessings after eating by one person can exempt others. T. provides classical theoretical examples to work out the law. As we recall, M. is concerned with an entirely different set of questions – who can join the quorum and under what circumstances one can be counted in the quorum to recite the invitation to say the blessings after the meal.

Most of the material supplements M. T. 5:21 starts a unit of single independent supplements drawn together from different contexts.

7:1

A. Three who ate together are obligated [to designate one person among them] to invite [the others at the meal to recite together the blessings over the meal].

B. One who ate

(1) דמאי [doubtfully tithed produce], or

(2) first tithe from which heave-offering was taken, or

(3) second tithe or הקדש [produce given to the Temple] which has been redeemed, or

(4) the servant who ate an olive's bulk [of food], or

(5) the Samaritan [who ate together with Israelites], may be counted [for the quorum] for extending the invitation [to recite together the blessings over the meal].

C. But one who ate

(1) טבל [untithed produce], or

(2) first tithe from which heave-offering was not taken, or

(3) second tithe or הקדש which had not been redeemed, or

(4) the servant who ate less than an olive's bulk, or

(5) the Gentile may not be counted [for the quorum] for extending the invitation [to recite together the blessings over the meal].

M. first sets out the basic assumption of the chapter. With a quorum of at least three, the participants at the conclusion of a meal must appoint a leader to call the group together with the appropriate formula to recite the meal blessings. This process is called זימון. The invitation itself is called the blessing of the זימון.

The structure and composition of the lists at B-C of persons who may or may not be counted in the quorum are a bit complex. B presents a composite list of five persons who can be counted in the quorum. The first three on the list are persons who ate either doubtfully tithed produce, or first tithe from which heave offering was removed, or sancta which was redeemed. Only the first item on this list really needs to be specified here. The other two are categories of foods which have been properly prepared for consumption. They probably appear in B's list only to balance out their counterparts on the list below at C.

A person in the fourth category on B's list, the servant who ate an olive's bulk of food, may be counted even though he does not sit together with the others at the meal. The Samaritan, the fifth grouping on M.'s list, also may be counted even though he is not considered to be a complete Israelite.

C's catalogue neatly balances B's list. An individual in C's first category, one who ate טבל, obviously cannot be counted because a person who ate untithed produce certainly should not be included in the quorum of the table fellowship. But as we said, this listing balances B's initial entry, one who ate דמאי (doubtfully tithed produce), who may be counted. M. continues, telling us that one who ate food which is partially prepared for use, from which, for instance, first tithe was taken, or food which was dedicated to the Temple but not yet redeemed, may not be counted in the quorum of the fellowship.

The last two entries on C's list are people obviously not to be included in the quorum. The gentile cannot be counted nor can one who has not eaten at least the minimum amount of food (cf. M.7:2B-C). Apparently M. includes these two entries to balance the last two categories on the list at B leaving us, in the end with two units of five elements, a convenient and common Mishnaic convention.

T. 5:14

A. All are obligated to [recite] the blessing [= grace] after the meal: (1) priests, (2) Levites, and (3) Israelites, (4) proselytes, and (5) freed slaves, (6) unfit priests, (7) נתינים, (8) ממזרים, (9) eunuchs castrated by man or born without testicles, (10) one whose testicles are crushed or whose male member has been cut off [cf. Deut. 23:1]—all of these are obligated [themselves],

B. but they can [ed. princ. lacks: not, by reciting,] exempt others from their obligation [to recite the blessing after the meal].

C. A person with underdeveloped genitals [whose sex is doubtful; טומטום] and a person who exhibits traits of both sexes [viz., an androgyne] are obligated [to recite],

D. but they cannot exempt others from their obligation [to recite].

T. 5:15

A. An androgyne can exempt its own kind [viz., one who is similarly androgynous] but cannot exempt any other kind [viz., a regular male or female, from the obligation to recite the blessing after meals].

B. A person of doubtful sexual traits can exempt neither its own kind nor any other kind [from this obligation].

T. 5:16

A. One who is half slave and half free-man can exempt neither his own kind nor any other kind [from this obligation].

M. is interested in defining who may be counted in the quorum so that one member may extend the invitation to others to recite collectively the blessing of the meal. T.'s autonomous supplements to M. emphasize two related concerns which M. does not address: one's inherent obligation to recite the blessing over the meal, and one's ability to exempt others from their obligation to recite through his own recitation of the meal blessings.

5:14A, ten categories of persons, is not a single unitary list. The first five are self-evidently obligated to recite the blessing of the meal. The remaining five, children of improper unions (6-8), or persons with defective bodily organs (9-10), might be obligated.

According to all manuscripts, B says that the preceding categories cannot exempt others from their obligation to recite the blessings over the meal. Lieberman's solution is to accept the reading of the first edition, "They can exempt others from their obligation." But this just begs the question. If all these people are obligated and can exempt others, there is nothing extraordinary about them, why bother to list them in the first place?

It may perhaps be better to split the catalogue into two lists. The first five are types who are obviously obligated to recite the meal blessings. The second five are obligated but *cannot* exempt others because of their unfortunate lineage or physical defect.

C-D then adds another two categories of people whose sex cannot be determined who are obligated to recite but cannot exempt others. 5:15 adds that androgyne with both male and female sex organs may exempt their own kind. The טומטום, who altogether lacks sexual signs, cannot even exempt others of this category. 5:16 adds further that one who falls into another liminal classification, a half-slave, half-free man, also falls outside of the ordinary taxonomy and cannot exempt others like himself.

7:2

A. Women, slaves, or minors [who ate together with adult Israelite males] may not be counted [in the quorum] for extending the invitation [to recite the blessings over the meal].

B. What is the minimum amount [that one must eat] so that he may be counted [in the quorum] for extending the invitation [to recite the blessings over the meal]?

C. At least an olive's bulk.

D. R. Judah says, "At least an egg's bulk."

M. lists three categories of individuals, women, slaves, and minors, who have inadequate status in the community. They therefore may count them in the quorum for the invitation to recite the blessing after the meal (A). B presents another rule concerning the minimum quantity that one must eat to be a part of the meal. Judah glosses at D. He requires that one eat a slightly larger quantity.

7:3

A. How do they invite [the others eating with them to join together to recite the blessings after the meal]?

B. (1) For three [who ate together the leader] says, "Let us recite the blessings." For three [others] and himself he says, "Recite the blessings."

C. (2) For ten he says, "Let us recite the blessings to our God." For ten and himself he says, "Recite the blessings [to our God]."

D. The same [rule applies] for ten or for ten thousand.

E. (3) For one hundred he says, "Let us recite the blessings to the Lord our God." For one hundred and himself he says, "Recite the blessings."

F. (4) For one thousand he says, "Let us recite the blessings to the Lord our God, God of Israel." For one thousand and himself he says, "Recite the blessings."

G. (5) For ten thousand he says, "Let us recite the blessings to the Lord our God, God of Israel, God of Hosts, who sits on the cherubim, for the food we have eaten." For ten thousand and himself he says, "Recite the blessings."

H. And as he recites the blessings, so do they answer after him, "Blessed be the Lord our God, God of Israel, God of hosts, who sits on the cherubim, for the food we have eaten."

I. R. Yose the Galilean says, "The [form of the] blessing they recite depends on the size of the congregation, as it says, 'Bless God in the Great Congregation, the Lord, O you who are of Israel's fountain' [Ps. 68:27]."

J. Said R. Aqiba, "What do we find [concerning the form of the call to recite the Prayer] in the synagogue? Whether there are many or few they say, 'Recite the blessings to the Lord.'" [The same rule should apply for the collective recitation of the blessings after the meal.]

K. R. Ishmael says, "[The form of the call to Prayer is:] 'Recite the blessings to the Lord who is blessed.'"

M. deals here with the text of the call to say grace. What is the formula they use for the invitation to recite the blessings of the meal? B-G gives us a succession of formulae. Each adds phrases for the leader to say as he calls on a group increasing in size. H says that the group responds in kind to the one who calls them to recite the blessings. Yose the Galilean's statement at I justifies the concept inherent in the preceding list of formulae. The invitation changes according to the size of the group.

Aqiba's statement, with Ishmael's accompanying gloss, J-K, makes a simple point. Once they have a minimum of ten participants the opening formula of the invitation should be fixed even if the group grows. They should not sometimes say, "Let us recite the blessings," and at other times say, "Recite the blessings." Rather they should act as they do in the synagogue and use one opening formula for all occasions.

T. 5:17

A. Women and slaves and children are exempt [from the obligation] [cf. M. Ber. 3:3, 7:2],

B. and cannot exempt others from their obligation [to recite the blessing after meals].

C. Indeed they said, "A woman may recite the blessing on behalf of her husband, a son may recite the blessing of behalf of his father, a slave may recite the blessing on behalf of his master."

T. 5:18

A. A minor who can eat an olive's bulk [of food at one sitting] may be counted [in the quorum of three men required] for extending the invitation [to recite the blessing after meals],

B. [but] one [a minor] who cannot eat an olive's-bulk may not be counted [in the quorum] for extending the invitation [to recite the blessing after meals].

C. One is not strict regarding [the inclusion of] a minor [who cannot eat an olive's bulk in the quorum for the invitation to recite the grace].

D. Whether one said, "Let us recite the blessings," [not counting the minor], or "Recite the blessings," [because they do include in the quorum a minor who cannot eat an olive's bulk] they do not take him to task for it.

E. But the overscrupulous take him to task for it [i.e. for counting in the quorum a minor who cannot eat an olive's bulk].

T. does not discuss directly whether women, slaves, and minors may be counted in the quorum. Instead T. continues with its own concerns parallel to M.'s. Persons in these three categories are free from the obligation to recite the blessings after the meal and may not exempt others through their recitation (A-B). C provides an unusual qualification of the ruling of A-B. A woman may exempt her husband through her recitation. A child may exempt his father and a slave may exempt his master.

5:18 directly supplements M. 7:2A. A minor who eats the minimum quantity at a meal may be counted in the quorum so that they may extend the invitation to recite the blessings after the meal. C's gloss adds that they are not strict with those who count a minor in the quorum. D-E spells this out.

Alternatively, one may interpret that D-E supplements M. 7:3. In spite of what M. says, in effect, T. says it should make no difference whether the person who recites the invitation says "Recite" or "Let us recite."

7:4

A. Three who ate together are not permitted to separate [to recite the meal blessings because if they do so they will not have the minimum quorum of three needed to be able to extend to others the invitation to recite together the blessings after the meal.]

B. And so too four, and so too five [who are eating together may not separate because if they do, some of them will not be able to recite the blessings after the meal with a quorum.]

C. Six [or more] may separate [into two groups of at least three each] until they reach ten.

D. Ten [or more] may not separate [because they invoke the name of God in the invitation that they recite with the more substantial quorum of ten, and if they separate, some will not be able to recite the meal blessings with the fuller invitation formula] until they reach twenty [then they may separate into two groups of ten].

7:5

A. Two groups [of people] eating in the same house, may combine together for זימון [to designate one representative to invite members of both groups to recite the meal blessings only] if some members of each group can see one another.

B. But if not, each group by itself [designates its own representative who] invites [the others in the group to recite together the blessings].

C. "And they may not recite the blessing over the wine [which they drink] unless they dilute it with water," the words of R. Eliezer.

D. And sages say, "They may recite [the blessing even over undiluted wine which they drink]."

Dissolution of the required quorum is M.'s concern. If the group splits up they may lose the number needed for the quorum and not be able to extend the invitation to collectively recite the blessings over the meal (7:4). M. therefore specifies that three may not separate but six or more may split into two groups of at least three. Ten may not separate into groups of three because then the quorum moves down in status one rung and, at the lower level, they recite a different formula.

M. also gives the reverse of this rule. Groups which ate separately may join together to form a larger quorum if they ate within sight of one another (7:5A-B).

The last unit, C-D, appears to be an appendage to the chapter. This dispute is over the kind of wine either to be used when reciting the meal blessing or for the Prayer of Sanctification or for other purposes. This serves as a transition to the next chapter which starts with a dispute over the blessing for the wine on Sabbath eve.

T. 5:19

A. Twenty [men] may be divided [into two smaller groups of ten, for purposes of reciting the blessing after meals] [cf. M. Ber. 7:4],

B. as long as none among them will [use this as an excuse to] exclude himself from the quorum [זימון].

T. 5:20

A. Rabban Simeon b. Gamaliel says, "If they had gotten up [from their chairs] and reclined [on the couches], and one has dipped with them [i.e., partaken of appetizers with them]–

B. "even though he did not eat an olive's-bulk of breadstuff with them, they may count him [in the quorum] for extending the invitation [to recite the blessings after the meal]."

T. 5:21

A. A gentile who recites a blessing using the name [of God]—one may respond [to his blessing by saying] "Amen."

B. [A gentile who praises] the name [of God]—[E. *ed. princ.:* A Samaritan who recites a blessing using the name of God–] one may not respond "Amen" to his blessing,

C. unless he has heard the entire blessing [cf. M. Ber. 8:8].

T. 5:22

A. One who was about to offer meal-offerings in Jerusalem says, "Blessed art Thou, O Lord,...who has brought us to this time."

B. When he offers them he says, "Blessed art Thou, O Lord,...who has sanctified us through his commandments and commanded us to offer meal-offerings."

C. When he eats them he says, "[Blessed art Thou, O Lord...] who brings forth bread from the earth."

D. One who was about to offer [animal] sacrifices in Jerusalem says, "Blessed [art Thou, O Lord...] who has sanctified us through his commandments and commanded us to offer sacrifices."

F. And when he eats them he says, "Blessed [art Thou, O Lord...] who has sanctified us through his commandments and commanded us to eat sacrifices."

T. 5:23

A. Ten people who were travelling on the road [and eating], even if they all eat from the same loaf, each recites the blessings [after the meal] for himself.

B. If they [stopped travelling and] sat down and ate [together], even if each eats from his own loaf, one person recites the blessings for the meal on behalf of all of them.

T. 5:24

A. Laborers who were working with the householder [and stopped to eat], lo, they recite two [blessings after eating].

B. [They say] the first blessing and then include the [third blessing] concerning Jerusalem in [their second] concerning the Land and conclude [their second blessing with the usual conclusion for the second blessing] concerning the Land.

C. But if they were working with him [as servants] during a meal [and eating along with him]

D. or if the householder was [eating with them and] reciting the blessing for them,

E. lo, they recite [the regular] four blessings.

5:19 glosses M. 7:4. They may separate into smaller groups as long as no one drops out on that account. T. then continues with a related supplement to M. According to Simeon b. Gamaliel (5:20) they may count in the quorum even one who joins the meal who just dips and eats small amounts of food with them, even if that amounts to less than the olive's bulk prescribed in M. 7:2B.

T. 5:21 follows, out of place here. It apparently just restates M. 8:8. 5:22-23 closely parallels T. 6:14-15 and probably belongs together with that unit. It deals with the blessings one recites when he eats meal-offerings. But it has some tangential relevance here at the end of the two chapters on food and meal blessings. C refers to the blessing, "He who brings forth bread from the earth."

5:23 is also autonomous of the present context. Its subject is whether those who eat while they are out travelling on the road must recite the blessings for the meal together as a group. It is relevant to our chapter because it rules that one person may recite the blessing over the meal on behalf of all those travellers who sat to eat together.

5:24, the final autonomous supplement in this unit, presents rules for domestic laborers. They recite only two, not four, blessings for the meal. But if they serve together with the householder (e.g., as waiters) they recite the entire four blessings after the meal. This pericope apparently indirectly supplements M. 7:1 which mentions the role of the servant informing the quorum for the invitation to recite the blessings of the meal.

Chapter Eight

BERAKHOT CHAPTER EIGHT
Houses Disputes Regarding the Dinner

This chapter is formally distinctive within its immediate context in our tractate. Disputes between the Houses of Hillel and Shammai make up almost this entire chapter. In subject matter as well it is loosely related to its context. As the protasis of 8:1 says, the disputes all relate in some way to the dinner. Some of these items relate to blessings. That interest provides a general thematic link to the other materials of Berakhot.

First, at 8:1, the Houses dispute the order of blessings at the Friday evening meal. This is followed, at 8:2, by a dispute over the order of washing hands and preparing the wine for the dinner. The next dispute, 8:3, concerns the proper place to set the napkin during the meal. The fourth unit, 8:4, deals with the order of cleaning and washing after the meal.

At 8:5 the Houses disagree over the order of the blessings of the Prayer of Division which coincides with the meal on Saturday night. They also disagree there over the formula for the blessing one recites over the light, an issue not necessarily related to the dinner. This brings with it further rulings, but not in the form of a Houses' dispute, on the subject of the blessings for the light and spices in the Prayer of Division ceremony.

Finally in 8:7-8 the chapter concludes with two rulings on the blessings for the meal. Where does one recite the meal blessings if, after eating, he forgot and left the meal without reciting? Must he return to the place of the meal or may he recite the blessing wherever he remembers? And last, what is the procedure for reciting the blessing over the meal if the group procured one cup of wine after the meal was over? Do they first recite the meal blessing or first say the blessing over the wine? A single independent ruling on the recitation of the response "Amen" to a blessing closes the chapter.

Overall this chapter is an excellent example of a unit whose coherence depends not so much on the tight adherence to a common theme, but mostly on a shared literary pattern, the Houses' dispute. None of the other chapters in this tractate evinces such clearly coherent external formulary traits. Accordingly, this chapter, an unusual and interesting work of redaction, shows a striking alternative way to join together related traditions on a common theme.

Based on the assumption that the attributions of these disputes are indeed accurate, we conclude that the several topics here treated may be traced back to the time of the first century masters. This chapter has the Houses talking about the recitation of blessings over wine and over the Sabbath day. It attributes to the Houses a concern with the order of actions at the fellowship meal (washing, mixing the wine), and with uncleanness and purity (placement of the napkin, cleaning the house). The Houses address issues related to the rituals of Prayer of Division at the conclusion of the Sabbath. They also dispute the formula for the blessing over the light in the Prayer of Division rituals. Finally the Houses speak of general issues regarding the blessings after the meal (where they recite the blessings, whether to recite the blessings over a cup of wine).

Given the diverse content of the chapter, let us reflect on the chapter's striking protasis. At the outset, this unit says that it joins together under the rubric of "the dinner" all these various issues regarding blessings, rituals, mealtime practice and Sabbath law. Apparently the editor who put these materials together thought that the dinner served as the common denominator for all of these materials, and should be the focus of this unit. This may be an echo of a much more important perception of the nature of the early rabbinic system. One redactor, possibly an early master, understood that the dinner, in other words the table fellowship, was a cardinal concern of the period of earliest rabbinic Judaism represented by the traditions of the Houses.

Tosefta takes up the task of systematically commenting on most of the pericopae of this chapter. 5:25-28 cite and comment on M. 8:1-4. T. 5:29 supplements M. with a related Houses' dispute. 5:30 presents an alternative version of M. 8:5A-B. Additional supplements at 5:31-32 round out the unit.

The Mishnah and Tosefta texts of this chapter are fully discussed in Neusner, *Invitation to the Talmud.*

8:1

A. These are the matters disputed by the House of Shammai and the House of Hillel concerning the dinner:

B. The House of Shammai say, "[In the Prayer of Sanctification at the dinner on the eve of the Sabbath or festival] they recite the blessing over [the Sabbath or festival] day, and then they recite the blessing over the wine."

C. And the House of Hillel say, "They recite the blessing over the wine, and then they recite the blessing over the day."

M.'s protasis, A, presents for the most part an accurate opening for the chapter. Except for a brief digression at 8:6, the disputes in this chapter all relate in one way or another to the dinner, or to the meal. The first dispute concerns the order of reciting the blessings at the Sabbath or festival meal on Friday evening or the eve of a festival. Because T.'s interpretation of the dispute is widely accepted by the commentators, we look immediately at the text of the relevant T. passage.

T. 5:25

A. *These are the matters disputed by the House of Shammai and the House of Hillel concerning the dinner:*

B. *The House of Shammai say, "[In the Prayer of Sanctification at the dinner on the eve of the Sabbath or festival] they recite the blessing over [the Sabbath or festival] day, and then they recite the blessing over the wine."*

C. [What is the basis of the House of Shammai's view? They reason that] one uses wine on account of the sanctity of the [Sabbath] day.

D. And one is obligated to recognize the sanctity of the day [through recitation of the Prayer of Sanctification of the Sabbath or festival] before he uses the wine.

E. *And the House of Hillel say, "They recite the blessing over the wine, and then they recite the blessing over the day."*

F. [And what is the basis of the House of Hillel's view? They reason that] the presence of wine [at the meal] allows a person to say the [blessing for the] sanctification of the day. [That is, without the wine there is no opportunity to recite the blessing for the day. Therefore one first recites the blessing over the wine.]

G. Another explanation [to support the view of the House of Hillel]: The [blessing over the] wine is a frequent action. The [sanctification blessing over the day] is not a frequent action. [And the principle is—that which is more frequent takes precedence in the order of performance].

H. And the *halakhah* follows the opinion of the House of Hillel.

T. explains the dispute in M. The House of Shammai gives priority to the blessing over the Sabbath day, the Prayer of Sanctification. The House of Hillel says that they recite the blessing first over the wine because the Prayer of Sanctification is dependent on the cup of wine. The wine is of paramount importance because they do not recite the Prayer of Sanctification unless there is wine. So one recites first the blessing over the wine.

8:2

A. The House of Shammai say, "They wash their hands [before beginning the meal], and then they mix the cup [of concentrated wine with water to prepare it for drinking]."

B. And the House of Hillel say, "They mix the cup, and then they wash their hands."

This is another dispute over the order of actions at the dinner. Again we look at T.'s explanation.

T. 5:26

A. *The House of Shammai say, "They wash their hands [before beginning the meal], and then they mix the cup [of concentrated wine with water to prepare it for drinking]."*

B. [What is the basis for the [ruling of] the House of Shammai? They first wash their hands] so they do not render the liquids on the sides of the cup unclean [by contact] with their hands, which in turn [through contact] could render [the outside of] the cup unclean.

C. *And the House of Hillel say,* [We reject the Shammaite position because we hold the view that] the outside of the cup is perpetually unclean. [Since the outside of the cup is already unclean, it makes no difference at what point one washes, whether before or after mixing the cup.]

D. [Why then must one wash after mixing the cup? The explanation is:] Another matter: One must juxtapose washing his hands with the recitation of the blessing [at the beginning of the meal]. [The act of mixing the cup may not intervene.]

According to T. and most subsequent interpreters, the underlying issue here is how to best keep the wine from becoming ritually unclean. The Shammaites say one washes his hands first to keep the liquids on the outside of the cup from becoming unclean and from rendering the wine unclean. The House of Hillel holds that it is impossible to protect the wine from some uncleanness. The outside of the cup is perpetually unclean. So this is not the determining factor in deciding the order of these actions. They base their view on the principle that one must not interrupt to mix the wine between washing his hands and beginning the meal.

8:3

A. The House of Shammai say, "[To avoid spreading uncleanness] one wipes his hands on a napkin and places it on the table."

B. And the House of Hillel say, "[He places the napkin] on the cushion."

The issue in this third pericope ostensibly seems to be a question of proper etiquette. During the meal where does one put the napkin? But here, once again, T. and all others see the issue of the dispute as a question of protecting the foods from uncleanness. T.'s commentary is clear.

T. 5:27

A. *The House of Shammai say, "[To avoid spreading uncleanness] one wipes his hands on a napkin and places it on the table.*

B. [What is the basis for the House of Shammai's view? He must put the napkin on the table] so that the liquid in the napkin does not become unclean through contact with the cushion, and in turn render unclean the person's hands.

C. *And the House of Hillel say, "[He places the napkin] on the cushion]."* [The principle is that] in all cases where there is doubt [whether there was contact between unclean] liquids and one's hands, [the law is that one's hands are considered] clean. [Here there is doubt whether the cushion is unclean, and whether the liquid in the napkin becomes unclean and renders one's hands unclean.]

D. Another explanation: [According to the House of Hillel there is no need to maintain clean] hands in order to eat unconsecrated food.

E. Rather, *"[He wipes his hand on the napkin and places it] on the cushion."*

F. Lest the liquids in the napkin become unclean through contact with the table and in turn render the food [on the table] unclean.

The House of Shammai fears that one will put his napkin on the cushion where it will become unclean and then render one's hands unclean. The Hillelites reject this view on several counts. First they doubt whether the cushion is unclean, and whether the wet napkin becomes unclean by touching it.

The Hillelites further believe that one need not worry about having unclean hands when he goes to eat unconsecrated ordinary foods. Now why then must he put the napkin on the cushion if these important concerns do not apply in this case? According to the Hillelites one must put it on the cushion, not on the table, lest it become unclean by touching the table and render unclean not one's hands, but the foods themselves.

8:4

A. The House of Shammai say, "[To avoid wasting food] they clean the house [and gather the scraps of food after the meal], and afterward wash their hands."

B. And the House of Hillel say, "They wash their hands, and afterward clean the house."

This seems to be an ordinary issue of household efficiency. Again T. interprets it as a dispute over purity laws.

T. 5:28

A. *The House of Shammai say, "[To avoid wasting food] they clean the house.*

B. [What is the basis for the House of Shammai's view? They clean the house first] so as not to waste food [by dripping water upon it when cleaning up after washing one's hands and thus rendering it susceptible to uncleanness].

C. *And afterward wash their hands.*

D. *And the House of Hillel say,* "If the servant is clever, he gathers up the pieces which are larger than an olive's bulk. [Then even if the scraps of food that remain become wet, and touch a source of uncleanness, they cannot become unclean, based on the principle that a scrap of food smaller than an olive's bulk cannot become unclean.]

E. *And they wash their hands and afterwards clean the house* [without concern over wasting food].

If water drips on food it becomes susceptible to uncleanness. The Shammaites caution against cleaning the foods up after washing one's hands because the food will become wet and may become unclean (hence wasted). The House of Hillel holds that an astute servant will gather up any pieces of food big enough to contract uncleanness. Then he may clean the house with wet hands without concern for rendering foods unclean.

8:5

A. The House of Shammai say, "[The order of the blessings in the service of the Prayer of Division when it is recited at the meal at the conclusion of the Sabbath is:] Light, meal, spices, Prayer of Division."

B. And the House of Hillel say, "[The order is:] Light, spices, meal, Prayer of Division."

C. The House of Shammai say, "[The formula for the blessing over the light is,] 'Who created the light of the fire.'"

D. And the House of Hillel say, "[It is,] 'Who creates the lights of the fire.'"

8:6

A. They recite a blessing [over the light or spices in the Prayer of Division Service at the conclusion of the Sabbath] neither over the light and spices of gentiles, nor the light and spices [used in honor] of the dead, nor the light and spices used before idolatry.

B. And they do not recite the blessing over the light [in the Prayer of Division Service at the conclusion of the Sabbath] until they make use of its illumination.

For the Prayer of Division one recites the blessings over the wine (not mentioned here), the light, the spices, and one says the Prayer of Division formulae themselves. This tangential unit asks, when the Prayer of Division is recited at the end of a meal on a Sabbath or festival night, what is the order of the blessings?

The first dispute here (A-B) concerns where one inserts the meal blessing into this complex of blessings. Judah in T. 5:30 presents an alternative version of the dispute (see below). The Houses also disagree on the proper formula for the blessing over the light (C-D). Further rules follow (8:6) governing the practice of reciting a blessing over the light and spices.

T. 5:29

A. The House of Shammai say, "One holds the cup of wine in his right hand, and the perfumed oil in his left hand.

B. "And he says the blessing over the cup of wine, and then he says the blessing over the perfumed oil."

C. And the House of Hillel say, "One holds the perfumed oil in his right hand, and the cup of wine in his left hand.

D. "And he says the blessing over the perfumed oil, and smears it on the head of his servant.

E. "And if the servant is a disciple of the sages, he smears it on the wall.

F. "For it is not befitting a disciple of the sages to go outside perfumed."

One may use perfumed oil instead of spices at the Prayer of Division service. This supplementary unit presents another Houses' dispute over the procedure for the Prayer of Division. In which hand does one hold the oil and in which does one hold the wine? Apparently this dispute is not perfectly balanced. D should parallel B and conclude, "And then one recites the blessing over the wine." But this last part of the line appears to be missing. Instead T. jumps to another subject–where to apply the oil. According to both Houses they smear the oil so that they can smell its aroma. They usually place it on the head of the servant (so that he can pass among the guests and they can all smell it). If the servant is a disciple of the sages he is not compelled to assume this task. They then smear the perfume instead on the wall of the room.

T. 5:30

A. Said R. Judah, "The House of Shammai and the House of Hillel did not dispute [concerning the order of the blessings at the meal at the conclusion of the Sabbath] that the blessing for the meal comes first, and the Prayer of Division comes last.

B. Concerning what did they dispute? [They disputed over the order of the blessings] for the light and the spices.

C. For the House of Shammai say, "Light and then spices."

D. And the House of Hillel say, "Spices and then light."

E. One who enters his house after the end of the Sabbath recites the blessing over the wine, the light, the spices and [then] recites [the] Prayer of Division.

F. And if he has but one cup [of wine], he sets it aside until after the meal and strings together all [these blessings] after it [i.e., after the blessing for the meal].

G. One recites Prayer of Division at the end of the Sabbath, and at the end of festivals, and at the end of the Day of Atonement, and at the end of the Sabbath [which immediately precedes] a festival, and at the end of a festival [preceding] the intermediate days of the festival.

H. One who is fluent [or, accustomed to doing so] recites many "Divisions" [i.e., enumerates many kinds of separations in his Prayer of Division, e.g., "Blessed art Thou, O Lord...(1) who separates the holy from the profane, (2) who separates Israel from the nations, (3) who separates light from darkness...," etc.],

I. and one who is not fluent recites one or two.

J. In the house of study–the House of Shammai say, "One [person] recites the blessings on behalf of all,"

K. and the House of Hillel say, "Each one recites the blessings for himself."

At A-D Judah presents a version of the Houses' dispute in M. 8:5A. In this version the issue between the Houses is the order of the blessings over the spices and the light.

The unit adds four autonomous rules to supplement M. E-F gives another alternative procedure for one who returns home to recite the blessings of the Prayer of Division service. G lists the days on which they say the Prayer of Division. H-I speaks of the custom of reciting different formulae in the liturgy of the Prayer of Division service. J-K concludes with a Houses' dispute concerning the practice of reciting the Prayer of Division in the study hall.

T. 5:31

A. [They do not recite the blessing over] a light whose source is hidden by a garment, or in a lamp,

B. [or for any light] where they see the flame, but cannot make use of its illumination,

C. or can make use of its illumination, but cannot see the flame.

D. They recite the blessing over it only if they both can see the flame, and make use of its illumination.

E. Over a lantern, even if it was not extinguished [i.e., it burned throughout the Sabbath], they may recite the blessing over it [for the light used in the Prayer of Division Service at the end of the Sabbath].

F. A light belonging to gentiles, one may not recite a blessing over it.

G. [At the end of the Sabbath in the Prayer of Division Service, they may recite the blessing over the light of] an Israelite who lit from a gentile, or of a gentile who lit a light from an Israelite's flame, they may recite [a blessing] over it.

H. From what time may one recite the blessing over it [the light]?   After nightfall.

I. If he did not recite the blessing [immediately] after nightfall, he may recite it throughout the night.

J. If he did not recite the blessing [at anytime] throughout the night, he may not recite it thereafter.

K. Fire and mules, though not actually created in the six days of creation,

L. were thought of [by God] during the six days of creation.

M. R. Yose says, "The fire of Gehenna was created on the second day and will never be extinguished, as it says, 'And they shall go forth and look on the dead bodies of the men that have rebelled against me, for their worm shall not die, their fire shall not be quenched, and they shall be an abhorrence to all flesh [Isa. 66:24].'"

A-D supplements M. 8:6B with rules governing the recitation of the blessing over the light. E-G provides further laws on the kind of light one may use (a glowing coal, the light of a gentile). H-J specifies the time of night for the recitation of the blessings. K-M refers to the creation of fire–the event symbolically represented in the rekindling of the light at the Prayer of Division service.

T. 5:32

A. The fire and spices of a bathhouse–one may not recite the blessing over them.

B. One who was standing in a spice dealer's store all day long recites the blessing [over spices] only once [cf. T. Ber. 6:15].

C. [If] he was continually going in and out, he recites the blessing each and every time [that he enters and smells the spices afresh].

5:32 adds two more rules to supplement M. 8:6. They may not use the fire or spices of the bathhouse for the Prayer of Division (A). This section of T. concludes with a general rule concerning the blessing one recites over the aroma of the spices. Where one constantly smells the fragrance, he recites the blessing only once.

8:7

A. He who ate [a meal] and forgot, and did not recite the blessing [over the meal and left the place where he ate the meal]:

B. The House of Shammai say, "He must go back to his place [where he ate] and recite the blessing."

C. And the House of Hillel say, "He may recite the blessing in the place he remembers."

D. And until when [after the meal] may he recite the blessings?

E. Until he digests the food.

This dispute varies the literary form of our chapter by starting with an independent protasis (A). The question is where must one recite the meal blessings if he forgot to do so at the conclusion of the meal and got up and left the place where he ate? D-E looks at a related issue. How long after the meal may one recite the blessings?

8:8

A. If they obtained wine after finishing the meal and they had only one cup:

B. The House of Shammai say, "They recite the blessing over the wine, and then they recite the blessing over the meal."

C. And the House of Hillel say, "They recite the blessing over the meal, and then they recite the blessing over the wine."

D. They may answer "Amen" after an Israelite who recites a blessing. But they do not answer "Amen" after a Samaritan who recites a blessing, unless they hear the entire blessing [and are certain that he did not say anything unacceptable in the blessing].

The premise of this last dispute is that where possible, one should recite the meal blessings over a cup of wine. The Houses dispute which blessing comes first, the blessing for the wine or the meal blessings.

A miscellaneous rule (D) about the propriety of responding "Amen" to a Samaritan's blessing concludes this chapter.

[T. 3:26 cites M. 8:8.]

Chapter Nine

BERAKHOT CHAPTER NINE
Blessings for Special Occasions

This chapter is a short collection of miscellaneous rules and traditions beginning with rules for blessings an individual recites on a number of special occasions. M. lists those blessings one recites upon seeing extraordinary events or places. First, a person who visits a national shrine or a place where they once worshipped idols, recites special blessings (9:1). One who sees meteorological or geological wonders also utters special blessings (9:2A-B). According to Judah one says a special blessing upon seeing the Mediterranean Sea, if he has not seen it for some time before (9:2C-D).

Next M. turns to blessings one recites for personal good fortune: for good or bad news or for the rains (9:2E-F) or for acquiring a new house or new clothes (9:3A). Concomitantly, M. cautions against misguided or vain personal prayers (9:3B-E). M. continues with rules for the prayers for a traveller (9:4).

The last pericope of the tractate, 9:5, is a complex composite of several parts. Its initial generalization obligates a person to recite a blessing when bad things happen. It follows this with a loosely related Scriptural passage and interpretation. At G, M. turns to a new concern. This coda to the chapter presents rules for behavior on the Temple Mount. One should act there with decorum, dress appropriately, not traverse the area as a shortcut to another place, and not spit in that place (9:5G-J). M. implicitly suggests these Temple rules to apply as well to behavior in the synagogue or any place one utters prayers or blessings.

Finally, M. concludes with a tradition about the response the people used to recite after hearing blessings in the Temple, also a basis for regulating parallel synagogue practice. This is followed by several loosely connected lines starting with a reference to a decree that people should invoke God's name when they greet their associates, which is supported with scriptural proof texts. Two further miscellaneous verses with a brief gloss close out the tractate.

This chapter yields little historical data. Its materials are mainly anonymous except for the attribution to Judah, an Ushan, of the rule concerning the blessing for seeing the sea (9:2C-D), and to Ben Azzai, a Yavnean, for the traveller's prayers (9:4B-C), and Nathan's final, rather cryptic gloss (9:5R).

T. explains and supplements M. adding Scriptural support for its rules and additional related regulations. In addition, T. greatly expands M.'s minimal catalogue of blessings for special occasions, first with additions at 6:3-6 and then with independent supplements at 6:9-15 regarding the blessings one recites for performing the actions associated with various commandments.

9:1

A. One who sees a place where miracles were performed for Israel says, "Blessed [art Thou, O Lord, our God, King of the Universe] who performed miracles for our forefathers in this place."

B. [One who sees] a place from which idolatry was uprooted says, "Blessed [art Thou, O Lord, our God, King of the Universe] who uprooted idolatry from our land."

9:2

A. For [seeing] meteors, and for earth tremors, and for lightning, and for thunder, and for the winds, one recites, "Blessed [art Thou, O Lord, our God, King of the Universe,] whose power fills the world."

B. For [seeing] the mountains, and for the hills, and for the seas, and for the rivers, and for the deserts, one recites, "Blessed [art Thou, O Lord, our God, King of the Universe,] the maker of [all of] creation."

C. R. Judah says, "One who sees the Mediterranean sea recites, 'Blessed [art Thou, O Lord, our God, King of the Universe,] who made the Mediterranean sea.'

D. "[He only recites this blessing] when he sees it [the sea] at intervals."

E. For the rains, and for good tidings, one recites, "Blessed [art Thou, O Lord, our God, King of the Universe,] who is good and does good."

F. And for bad tidings one recites, "Blessed [art Thou, O Lord, our God, King of the Universe,] the true judge."

This final chapter deals with blessings recited in special contexts. Up to this point, M. spoke of blessings as either components of the daily cycle of the liturgy or as formulae recited before and after eating. In this chapter we are told that one must recite blessings on other occasions as well. This unit first gives us a catalogue of five instances for which one recites a blessing of praise or thanksgiving (9:1-2). One says a blessing as a formula of thanksgiving when visiting a national shrine or a place from which idol-worship was eliminated. 9:2 provides blessings which one recites upon witnessing special natural events or geological wonders, or according to C-D, for viewing the sea.

In other instances one recites a special blessing. One recites a blessing of thanks upon hearing good news, and one recites a blessing of affirmation upon hearing bad news (9:2E-F). 9:3A adds the blessing of thanks which one says for new acquisitions, such as a new house or new clothes.

T. 6:1

A. The invitation to recite the blessing after meals has a scriptural basis.

B. As Scripture states, "And you shall eat and be full, and you shall bless [the Lord your God for the good land which he has given you]" (Deut. 8:10)–this [refers to] the invitation.

C. "...the Lord your God..." –this refers to the first blessing [of the blessings after the meal].

D. "...for the [good] land..."–this refers to the blessing for the Land [the second blessing of the series].

E. "...the good [land]..."–this refers to Jerusalem [the third blessing],

F. as it is said, "That goodly hill country and Lebanon" (Deut. 3:25).

G. "...which the Lord has given you..."–this refers to [the fourth blessing, which contains the words] "who is good and does good."

H. From what [scriptural verse do we learn] that just as you recite blessings after it [the meal], so you recite a blessing before it?

I. Scripture states, "Which he has given you"–[meaning] from the time that he gave you [food, i.e., at the beginning of the meal].

J. Whence [do we learn that one recites a blessing] also upon [seeing] mountains and hills?

K. Scripture states, "For the [good] land."

L. Whence [do we learn that one recites a blessing] also over the [study of] Torah and over [the performance of] the commandments?

M. Scripture states, "Which he has given you."

N. And Scripture states, "I will give you the tables of stone, [with the law and the commandments]" (Exod. 24:12).

O. R. Meir says, "Whence [do we learn] that just as you must praise [God] for the good [which befalls you] so must you praise [him] for the bad?" [Cf. M. Ber. 9:5, 9:3.]

P. "Scripture says, 'Which the Lord your God has given you':

Q. "'Your God [אלהיך]'–[this epithet connoting] your judge: whatever judgment he metes out to you, whether it be for good or for punishment."

T. 6:1 supplies a scriptural basis for many of the blessings discussed in our tractate, including those mentioned in M. 9:2A, 9:3B, and 9:5A. T. finds allusions to several blessings in Deut. 8:10–the blessing of the זימון (the invitation to recite the meal blessings, cf. Ch. 7), the four blessings of the meal, blessings before eating, blessings recited for seeing mountains and hills, blessings recited for the study of Torah and for the performance of other rituals (cf. T. 6:9-15, 5:2).

In a related tradition attributed to Meir (O-Q), T. uses the same verse to justify the ruling that one recites blessings over both good and bad things which happen.

T. 6:2

A. One who sees idolatry says, "Blessed [art Thou, O Lord, our God, King of the Universe,] who is slow to anger."

B. [One who sees] a place from which idolatry was uprooted says, "Blessed [art Thou, O Lord, our God, King of the Universe] who uprooted idolatry from our land."

C. "May it be thy will, Lord our God, that idolatry be uprooted from every place in Israel, and turn the hearts of thy servants to serve thee."

[Editio princeps adds: Outside the Land of Israel one need not recite this. For the majority of the inhabitants there are gentile.

R. Simeon says, "Even outside the Land of Israel one must recite this, for they are destined to convert.

As it says, "At that time I will change the speech of the people to a pure speech, that all of them may call on the name of the Lord and serve him with one accord (Zeph. 3:9)."]

D. One who sees a crowd says, "Blessed [art Thou, O Lord, our God, King of the Universe,] who knows the secrets.

E. Just as their faces are different one from the other, so are their opinions different one from the other."

F. When Ben Zoma saw crowds on the Temple Mount he would say, "Blessed is he who created all these people to serve me. How hard did Adam have to toil, before eating even a morsel. He first seeded, plowed, [weeded, irrigated,] reaped, made sheaves, threshed, winnowed, separated, grinded, sifted, kneaded, baked and only then could he eat a morsel. But I arise in the morning and find all this prepared before me.

G. "See how hard Adam toiled before he had a shirt to wear. He sheared, bleached, separated, dyed, spun, wove, [washed, sewed] and only then did he have a shirt to wear. But I arise in the morning and find all this prepared for me.

H. How many craftsmen must rise early and retire late [to prepare my food and clothing]. And I arise in the morning and find all this before me."

I. And so Ben Zoma would say, "What does a grateful guest say, 'Blessed be this householder. May we remember well this householder. How much wine did he bring before me! How many slices [of bread, meat] did he bring before me! How many cakes did he bring before me! [How much energy did he expend on my behalf.] He expended his energies only for me.

J. "But what does an ungrateful guest say? 'What did I take from this householder to eat or drink? I ate just one slice of his bread and drank just one cup of his wine. He expended his energies [to prepare the meal] only on behalf of his wife and children.'

K. And so [Scripture] says, 'Remember to extol his work, of which men have sung' [Job 36:24]. [Extol the efforts of your host in this world by reciting blessings over the food he provides for you.]

A-C supplements M. 9:1B adding a blessing which one recites for seeing an idol and additional phrases which one recites when he comes to a place from which idolatry was uprooted. D-E is an autonomous supplement which provides the formula of a blessing to be recited when one sees a crowd.

Ben Zoma's two related teachings follow at F-K. The first discusses the blessing he recited when he saw a crowd on the Temple mount. The second is Ben Zoma's homily of the blessing a good guest should bestow upon his host.

T. 6:3

A. One who sees a black, a red, or a white skinned person, or a hunchback, or a midget [E. *editio princeps* omits: or a deaf man, or an imbecile, or a drunk] says, "Blessed [art Thou, O Lord, our God, King of the Universe,] who changes the creatures."

B. [One who sees an] amputee, or a lame person, a blind person, or a person afflicted with boils says, "Blessed [art Thou, O Lord, our God, King of the Universe,] the true judge."

T. 6:4

A. One who sees handsome people or beautiful trees says, "Blessed [art Thou, O Lord, our God, King of the Universe,] who created handsome creatures in his world."

T. 6:5

A. One who sees a rainbow in the sky recites, "Blessed [art Thou, O Lord, our God, King of the Universe,] who is faithful in his covenant, who remembers the covenant."

T. 6:6

A. One who was walking between graves [in a cemetery] says, "Blessed [art Thou, O Lord...] ...who knows your number. He will judge you and he will resurrect you to judgment. Blessed [art Thou, O Lord...] whose word is trustworthy, who resurrects the dead."

B. One who sees the sun, or the moon, or the stars, or the constellations says, "Blessed [art Thou, O Lord...] maker of [all of] creation."

C. R. Judah says, "One who recites a blessing for the sun, behold this is heresy."

D. And so R. Judah would say, "If one sees the sea regularly, and something about it has changed, he must recite [a blessing]."

T. adds here a list of supplementary of blessings one recites upon seeing unusual things. One says a blessing when he sees deformed or afflicted people (6:3A), or a disabled person (B), or handsome people (6:4), beautiful trees (6:4), a rainbow (6:5). T. also gives us a blessing to be recited in a cemetery (6:6A).

6:6B adds to M. 9:2B's list of natural wonders. One recites a blessing for the sun, moon, stars or constellations, presumably if there is some special appearance to them. Judah's gloss asserts that one who recites a blessing over the sun is engaging in a heretical practice (perhaps suspected of sun-worship). At D Judah supplements his ruling (M. 9:2C-D) regarding the blessing one recites for seeing the Mediterranean.

9:3

A. One who built a new house, or bought new clothes says, "Blessed [art Thou, O Lord, our God, King of the Universe, who kept us alive, and sustained us, and] brought us to this occasion."

B. One recites a blessing over evil, as he would recite over good. And one recites a blessing over good, as he would recite over evil.

C. And one who cries out over a past occurrence, lo, this is a vain prayer.

D. How so? One whose wife was pregnant and he recited, "May it be thy will that she bear a male child," lo, this is a vain prayer.

E. One who was coming down the road, and he heard cries in the city and recited, "May it be thy will that these [cries] do not come from my house," lo, this is a vain prayer.

9:4

A. One who enters a town recites two prayers; one on his entry, and one on his exit.

B. Ben Azzai says, "[He recites] four [prayers], two on his entry, and two on his exit.

C. "He gives thanks for the past and cries out for the future [both upon his arrival and upon his departure]."

This section refers to an improper blessing, and a vain prayer (B-C). D-E spells out (with an illustration) the reference to a vain prayer. A person may not pray to change an event in the past, e.g. that his pregnant wife bear a male child. And a traveller may not pray that his family has not suffered any evil. Having mentioned the unacceptable prayers of the traveller who approaches a town, M. adds, the independent rule of 9:4, the prayers which a traveller may legitimately recite when he comes to a town.

9:5

A. A person is obligated to recite a blessing over bad fortune, just as he recites a blessing over good fortune.

B. As it says, "And you shall love the Lord your God with all your heart, and with all your soul, and with all you might" (Deut. 6:5).

C. "With all your heart"–with your two desires, with your desire for good, and with your desire for evil.

D. "With all your soul"–even if he takes your soul.

E. "With all your might"–with all your wealth.

F. Another interpretation: "With all your might [מאדך]"–for every measure [מידה] which he metes out for you [מודד לך], thank him [מודה לו] greatly [מאד מאד]. [This interpretation is based on a play on words.]

G. A person should not act frivolously opposite the Eastern Gate [of the Temple] for it faces the Chamber of the Holy of Holies.

H. One shall not enter the Temple mount with his walking stick, or with his overshoes, or with his money bag, or with dust on his feet.

I. And one should not use [the Temple mount] for a shortcut.

J. And spitting [while on the Temple mount is forbidden, based on an inference] from a קל וחומר [an argument a minori ad majus].

K. [At one time] they used to say, "Forever," at the conclusion of all blessings recited in the Temple.

L. After the heretics tried to corrupt [the tradition] by saying, "[Based on what you say,] there is only one world [and no afterlife in the world to come]," they ordained that one should say "Forever and ever."

M. And they ordained that a person should greet his associate with God's name.

N. As it says, "And behold Boaz came from Bethlehem and he said to the reapers, 'The Lord be with you!' And they answered, 'The Lord bless you'" (Ruth 2:4).

O. And [as further support for this practice] it says, "[The angel greeted Gideon saying,] 'The Lord be with you mighty man of valor' (Judges 6:12).

P. And it says, "[Harken to your father for he gave birth to you and] do not despise your mother when she is old" (Prov. 23:22).

Q. And it says, "It is time for the Lord to act, for thy law has been broken" (Ps. 119:126).

R. [In K's margin: R. Nathan says, "Thy law has been broken. It is time 'to act' for the Lord."]

This last unit of the tractate is a long composite. 9:5A provides a justification for the rules of 9:2E-F, that one recites blessings over both good and bad tidings. This unit's exegesis of a verse from the Scriptural passages of the *Shema* (Deut. 6:4), appropriately closing the tractate with a reference to the subject with which it opened, the *Shema*.

The interpretation at C best supports M.'s point in A. One must thank God with a blessing for whatever destiny he allots a person, whether good or evil.

The remainder of this pericope is a assortment of material which serves as a coda to the tractate as a whole. The items which relate to etiquette on the Temple mount (G-J) are pertinent here because the redactor meant us to apply them to the setting of the synagogue or other place of prayer. The implicit point is that one must treat the locale of prayer as if it was the Temple.

The remaining materials are elliptical, their meaning is unclear, and their relationship to the present context not wholly evident. K tells us that in the Temple they used to respond with a certain formula to the blessings recited there. Later that formula had to be revised by a decree. M adds that it was further ordained that one must use God's name in greeting his associate and cites scriptural proof to support this practice.

While neither one of these traditions has any direct relevance to our context, one might argue that together they indirectly allude to the power of later authorities both to revise earlier rules for reciting blessings and to decree new instances for the invocation of God's name. On the basis of this concept, the rabbis substantiate and sanction the entire system of blessings laid out in this tractate. Accordingly, these last traditions, ostensibly out of context, provide important precedents as a justification for the practices discussed throughout M. Berakhot.

P and Q are difficult to interpret in their context. They perhaps gloss K-M to declare that innovations must not be taken lightly, but when circumstances make it necessary, one must issue a new decree and ordain a new set of practices. This serves as a final allusion to the elaborate system of rabbinic prayers and blessings, established in totality after the Temple was destroyed between the first and third centuries.

T. 6:7

A. R. Meir says, "Behold Scripture states, 'And you shall love the Lord your God with all your heart–[that means] with both of your impulses: with the good impulse and with the evil impulse' [M. Ber. 9:5].

B. "And with all your soul–even if he takes your soul" [M. Ber. 9:5].

C. "And thus Scripture states, 'For thy sake we are slain all day long' (Ps. 44:23 [= RSV 44:22])."

D. Another interpretation: "And with all your soul"–with each and every soul that was created in you.

E. As it is written, "Let my soul live [that I may praise thee]" (Ps. 119:175). And Scripture states, "All my bones shall say, 'O Lord who is like thee?'" (Ps. 35:10).

F. Ben Azzai says, "'With all your soul'–give your soul for the [observance of the] commandments."

G. There are [kinds of] prayers which are considered frivolous [uttered in vain].

H. How so? [If] one gathered in one hundred measures [of produce], [and] said [as a prayer], "May it be [thy] will that there be [here] two hundred,"

I. [or if] he gathered in one hundred barrels, [and] said, "May it be [thy] will that there be [here] two hundred," lo, this is an idle prayer [uttered in vain].

J. But he [may rather] pray that what he brings in may be for a blessing and not for a curse [viz., that it should not spoil] [cf. M. Ber. 9:3].

T. 6:8

A. R. Dosetai ben R. Yannai said in the name of R. Meir, "Lo, Scripture states concerning Isaac, 'And I will bless you and multiply your seed for my servant Abraham's sake' (Gen. 26:24).

B. "Isaac expounded [this blessing] and said, 'Since a blessing is earned only through one's actions...,' he arose and sowed.

C. "As Scripture states, 'And Isaac sowed in that land and reaped in the same year a hundredfold' (Gen. 26:12)."

D. "A hundred"–in number. "A hundredfold"–[this means] one hundred piles [of produce]:

E. one hundred measures which were measured one hundred times. It turns out that there is one hundred for [each original] measure [i.e., one hundred times one hundred–a hundredfold].

A-F supplements M. 9:5B-E with alternative explanations of the verse and additional related materials. G-J supplements M.9:3D-E. It gives other cases of vain prayers and an example of a proper prayer. T. 6:8 continues with a tradition related to 6:7's reference to a crop which is blessed.

T. 6:9

A. One who performs any of the commandments must recite a blessing over them.

B. One who makes a *sukkah* for himself says, "Blessed [art Thou, O Lord...] who has brought us to this occasion."

C. [One who] enters to dwell in it says, "Blessed [art Thou, O Lord...] who has sanctified us through his commandments and commanded us to dwell in the *sukkah*."

D. Once he recites a blessing over it on the first day, he need not recite the blessing again [on the remaining days of the festival].

T. 6:10

A. One who makes a *lulab* for himself says, "Blessed [art Thou, O Lord...] who gave us life and preserved us and brought us to this occasion."

B. When he takes it [in hand] he says, "Blessed [art Thou, O Lord...] who gave us life and preserved us and brought us to this occasion."

C. And he must recite the blessing over it [the *lulab*] all seven [days of the festival].

D. One who makes fringes for himself [on his garment] says, "Blessed [art Thou, O Lord...] who has given us life..."

E. When he wraps himself [in the garment] he says, "Blessed [art Thou, O Lord...] who has sanctified us through his commandments and commanded us to wrap ourselves in fringes."

F. And he must recite a blessing over them [the fringes] every day [when he puts on the garment].

G. One who makes phylacteries [tefillin] for himself says, "Blessed [art Thou, O Lord...] who has given us life..."

H. When he puts them on [he says], "Blessed [art Thou, O Lord...] who has sanctified us through his commandments and commanded us to put on phylacteries."

I. When does he put them on? In the morning.

J. [If] he did not put them on in the morning, he may put them on [any time] throughout the entire day.

T. 6:11

A. He who slaughters [an animal] must recite a separate blessing [over his activity]. He says, "Blessed [art Thou, O Lord...who has commanded us] concerning slaughtering."

B. One who covers the blood must recite a separate blessing [over his activity]. He says, "Blessed [art Thou, O Lord...who has commanded us] concerning the covering of blood with dust."

T. 6:12

A. One who circumcises [an infant] must recite a separate blessing [over his activity]. He says, "Blessed [art Thou, O Lord...who has commanded us] concerning circumcision."

B. The father of the infant must recite a separate blessing [over his activity]. He says, "Blessed [art Thou, O Lord...who has commanded us] to bring him [i.e., the child] into the covenant of Abraham our father."

C. What do the bystanders [at the circumcision] say [to the father]? "Just as you brought him into the covenant, so may you raise him for [the study of] Torah, marriage, and good deeds."

T. 6:13

A. What does the one who recites a blessing [after the circumcision is performed] say?

B. [He says], ["Blessed art Thou, O Lord...] who sanctified the beloved [i.e., Isaac] from the womb and placed [the mark of] a statute in his flesh, and sealed his offspring with the sign of the holy covenant. As [our] reward for [having observed] this [commandment], O living God, our Portion and our Rock, now save the beloved of our flesh from destruction [i.e., let the wound heal and preserve the child's life]. Blessed [art Thou, O Lord,] who establishes the covenant."

[Ed. princ. adds: He who circumcises proselytes says, "(Blessed art Thou, O Lord...who has sanctified us) through his commandments and commanded us to circumcise proselytes, to cause the blood of the covenant to flow from them, for were it not for the blood of the covenant, the heavens and earth would not exist, as it is written, "If I have not established my covenant with day and night and the ordinances of heaven and earth" (Jer. 33:25). Blessed (art Thou, O Lord,) who establishes the covenant."

He who circumcises slaves says, "Blessed (art Thou, O Lord...) who has sanctified us through his commandments and commanded us concerning circumcision." The one who recites a blessing (after the circumcision is performed) says, "Blessed (art Thou, O Lord...) who has sanctified us through his commandments and commanded us to circumcise slaves and to cause the blood of the covenant to flow from them, etc."]

T. 6:14

A. One who was about to separate heave-offering and tithes [from his produce] says, "Blessed [art Thou, O Lord...] who has brought us to this occasion."

B. When he separates them he says, "Blessed [art Thou, O Lord...] who has sanctified us through his commandments and commanded us to separate heave-offering and tithes."

C. When does he recite the blessing over them? When he actually separates these [priestly gifts from the produce].

T. 6:15

A. Ten [individuals] who were performing ten [different] commandments [at the same time in each other's company]—each one must recite a blessing for himself.

B. [If] all were engaged in the performance of the same commandment—one [of them] may recite a blessing on behalf of them all.

C. An individual who was performing ten [different] commandments must recite a blessing over each one.

D. [If] he was performing one commandment throughout the day, he need recite the blessing only once.

E. [If] he was performing [the commandment] intermittently, he must recite a blessing over each [individual performance of the commandment].

This catalogue unpacks in detail T.'s earlier reference to the recitation of blessings with the performance of the commandments (cf. T. 6:1L). We have before us a long and repetitive list of various blessings to be recited for several ritual actions: making a sukkah and taking a lulab on the Sukkot festival, making and wearing fringes and tefillin, performing the rites of slaughtering an animal and of circumcising an infant (or, according to some MSS evidence, a proselyte), and for separating heave-offerings and tithes. Note that in several places (6:9, 6:10, and 6:14) T. says that one must recite the blessing, "Who brought us to this occasion," the blessing also mentioned at M. 9:3A.

Finally, T. 6:15 raises a separate question, concerning the economical use of blessings recited over commandments. (See also our discussion of T. 5:22-23 at the end of chapter seven, above.) T. asks whether one person may recite a blessing on behalf of another who is performing the same ritual. B says yes. D rules that one need not repeat the blessing each time he performs the same ritual. E qualifies this rule, adding that if there are interruptions between one act and the next, the blessing must be repeated.

T. 6:16

A. *One who enters a town recites two prayers, one on his entry and one on his exit.*

B. R. Simeon [Ben Azzai] says, "[He recites] four [blessings]: two on his entry and two on his exit."

C. He says, "May it be thy will, Lord my God, God of my fathers, that you bring me into this town in peace."

D. Once he has entered, he says, "I give thanks to thee, Lord my God, God of my fathers, that you brought me in in peace. So may it be thy will that you bring me forth in peace."

E. [When he is exiting he says, "May it be thy will, Lord my God, that you bring me forth in peace."] Once he has exited, he says, "I give thanks to thee, Lord my God, God of my fathers, that you brought me forth in peace. So may it be thy will to bring me to my house in peace."

T. 6:17

A. One who enters a bathhouse recites two prayers, one when he enters, one when he leaves.

B. Upon entering what does he say? "May it be thy will, Lord my God, to bring me in safely and bring me out safely, and let no accident befall me. And if, God forbid, an accident should befall me, may my death be atonement for my sins. And save me from this and similar [dangers] in the future."

T. cites and supplements M. 9:4, supplying for us the text of the prayers. T. 6:17 adds the rule concerning the prayers one recites upon entering a bathhouse.

T. 6:18

A. R. Judah says, "A person must recite three blessings each day: 'Blessed [art Thou, O Lord, our God, King of the Universe,] who did not make me a gentile'; 'Blessed [art Thou, O Lord, our God, King of the Universe,] who did not make me a boor'; 'Blessed [art Thou, O Lord, our God, King of the Universe,] who did not make me a woman.'

B. "[What is the basis in Scripture for these blessings? 'Blessed art Thou, O Lord, our God, King of the Universe, who did not make me] a gentile,' [because the gentiles are of no matter. As it says,] 'All the nations are as nothing before him' [Isa. 40:17].

C. "[Blessed art Thou, O Lord, our God, King of the Universe, who did not make] a boor,' for, *A boor does not fear sin* [M. Abot 2:5].

D. "[Blessed art Thou, O Lord, our God, King of the Universe, who did not make me] a woman, for women are not obligated to perform the commandments."

E. They drew a parable: to what is the matter similar [viz., the cases of gentiles, ignoramuses, and women performing commandments]? To a human king who said to his servant, "Cook a dish for me, and he [the servant] had never cooked a dish before. In the end he spoiled the dish and angered his master. [Or if he commanded the slave] to hem [so E. *ed. princ.]* a shirt for him, and he had never hemmed a shirt before. In the end he soiled the shirt and angered his master. [Thus those who are not properly schooled in the correct observance of the commandments should not attempt to perform them, lest their actions be an affront to God.]

In this an independent supplement to M., Judah lists three blessings which one must recite daily as part of the daily liturgy, not as blessings for seeing special things or for travel or the like. B-D provides support that justifies the recitation of these blessings. E gives us a parable to explain that only a person who is prepared to fulfill obligations (a learned Israelite man) may be expected to do so properly and to please his master.

T. 6:19

A. *One should not enter the Temple Mount* with money tied in his purse, *or with dust on his feet, or with his money-bag* [M. Ber. 9:5] girded to the outside [of his garments],

B. as Scripture states, "Guard your steps when you go to the house of the Lord" (Eccles. 4:17 [= RSV 5:1]).

C. R. Yose b. R. Judah says, "Lo Scripture states, 'For no one might enter the king's gate clothed with sackcloth' (Esther 4:2). How much more so then [regarding the abode of God]!"

D. *And spitting [is forbidden on the Temple Mount based on an inference] from a* וחומר קל[M. Ber. 9:5] [as follows]:

E. Now if [with respect to wearing] a shoe, which is not contemptuous, the Torah said, "Do not enter [the Temple Mount] wearing a shoe," how much more so is spitting, which is contemptuous, [to be forbidden on the Temple Mount].

T. cites and fills in M. 9:5H-J. Yose b. Judah, at C, supplements M. with a general statement and a verse. D-E spells out the argument of M. 9:5J.

T. 6:20

A. One who opens [his blessings] with [the invocation of the divine name] "Lord" and closes his blessing with the divine name "Lord,"

B. [V lacks B-E] lo, he is a sage.

C. [One who opens with the divine name] "Lord" and closes with "God,"

D. lo, he is a boor.

E. One who opens with "God," and closes with "Lord,"

F. lo, this is a middle way.

G. One who opens with "God," and closes with "God,"

H. lo, this is another way [heresy].

T. emphasizes the importance of the proper invocation of God's name in a blessing. A person who recites the wrong formula of a blessing may be classed a heretic or a boor. This autonomous T. relates to the mention in M. 9:5L of the heretics who corrupted the tradition, cited in the next T.-passage.

T. 6:21

A. [At one time] they used to say, "Forever," at the conclusion of all blessings recited in the Temple.

B. After the heretics tried to corrupt [the tradition] by saying, "[Based on what you say,] there is only one world [and no afterlife in the world to come],"

C. they ordained that one should say "Forever and ever."

D. They [did thereby] proclaim that this world is [related] to the next [world after death] as a vestibule is [related] to a great dining hall.

T. cites M. directly and adds a supplementary gloss at D.

T. 6:22

A. One did not respond "Amen" [after a blessing was recited] in the Temple.

B. Whence that they did not respond "Amen" in the Temple?

C. Scripture states, "[Then the Levites] said, 'Stand up and bless the Lord your God from everlasting to everlasting. Blessed be thy glorious name which is exalted above all blessing and praise'" (Neh. 9:5).

D. Whence that one must so respond to every blessing?

E. Scripture states, "Exalted above all blessing" (ibid).

F. [It applies] to every blessing and every [expression of] praise.

T. supplements M. 9:5K-L. A verse proves that in the Temple they did not answer with the formula "Amen."

T. 6:23

A. When Israel began forsaking the Torah, the elders would swallow it [the Tetragrammaton] up among them [viz., pronounce the name of God indistinctly, in greeting each other] [cf. M. Ber. 9:5],

B. as Scripture states, "And behold, Boaz came from Bethlehem; [and he said to the reapers, 'The Lord be with you!' And they answered, 'The Lord bless you]' (Ruth 2:4).

C. "And Scripture states, 'The Lord is with you, mighty men of valor'" (Judg. 6:12).

D. And Scripture states, "Do not despise your mother when she is old" (Prov. 23:22);

E. "It is time for the Lord to act" [read, "It is time to act for the Lord!"] (Ps. 119:126). [B-E = M. Ber. 9:5.]

T. appears to supplement M. 9:5N-Q but does not help us understand its meaning.

T. 6:24

A. Hillel the Elder used to say, "You should scatter at the time of gathering. And you should gather in at the time of scattering."

B. And so Hillel used to say, "When you see that the Torah is beloved to all Israel and all rejoice in it, the you must spread it about. And if this is not the case, then you must gather it in."

C. "as Scripture states, 'One man gives freely, yet grows all the richer' (Prov. 11:24).

D. "[But] when you see that the Torah is forsaken by Israel, and all are not careful about it, [then] gather it in [viz., preserve it among yourselves],

E. "as Scripture states, 'It is time for the Lord to act' (ibid.) [i.e., 'it is time to act for the Lord']."

F. R. Meir used to say, "There is no person is Israel who does not perform one hundred commandments each day [and recite blessings for them].

G. One recites the *Shema* and recites blessings before and after it. And one eats his bread and recites blessings before and after. And one recites the Prayer of Eighteen Blessings three times. And one performs all the other commandments and recites blessings for them."

T. 6:25

A. And so R. Meir used to say, "There is no person in Israel who is not surrounded by commandments.

B. [Every person wears] tefillin on his head, tefillin on his arm, and has a mezuzah on his door post, the mark of circumcision in his flesh, and four fringes on his garment around him."

C. So did David say, "Seven times a day I praise thee for thy righteous ordinances" (Ps. 119:164).

D. When one enters the bathhouse [and realizes that he is naked, he says, 'Woe is me for I am stripped of the commandments.' But] when he sees the mark of circumcision in his flesh he praises the Lord saying, "To the choirmaster according to the שמינית" (Ps. 12:1) [The eighth, שמינית, is an allusion to circumcision on the eighth day.]

E. And so he says, "The angel of the Lord encamps around those who fear him and delivers them" (Ps. 34:7).

The first part of this autonomous supplement, attributed to Hillel, makes reference to Psalms 119:126. Otherwise it is hardly relevant to the context. But the materials attributed to Meir serve as an appropriate conclusion to the tractate. Meir says that every Israelite, each day performs one hundred commandments and in so doing recites one hundred blessings. [Seven for the two recitations of the *Shema*, 57 for the three recitations of the nineteen blessings, at least five blessings before and after eating (= 69) plus the blessings for the other commandments one performs.]

As Meir saw it, each performance of a commandment and each recitation of a blessing was part of a coherent system of practice in the Israelite way of life. Our tractate's redactors in both M. and T. employed a parallel conception to lend coherence to the system of blessings and prayers as they joined together the disparate materials of our tractate, on the *Shema'*, the Prayer, the meal and food blessings, and other blessings.

The tractate concludes with the message of a simple homiletical pericope. One who keeps the commandments will be surrounded by them and will be protected by them.

Appendix

The Relationship between Mishnah and Tosefta

I. The Traits of T.

T. is a complex composite appendix to M. In effect it is a collection of three types of tannaitic materials woven together: (1) a commentary to M., a sort of proto-Talmud to our tractate; (2) an appendix which adds many related supplements to M. Ber.; (3) a collection of independent units of materials related in some general way to M. Ber.

The Tosefta to tractate Berakhot consists of six chapters according to the Vienna manuscript which Lieberman follows in his edition of T. The Erfurt manuscript isolates the materials which correspond to M. chapter eight, T. 5:25-32, as a separate, and seventh, chapter. Lieberman gives us 140 numbered pericopae in 568 lines. The average length of each pericope is 4 lines. The Tosefta tractate contains about 5600 words. T. is thus more than two times as long as M. Berakhot which, following Sack's edition, contains 58 numbered pericopae in 208 lines–approximately 2000 words. The average length of each M. pericope is then 3.5 lines.

If one reads T. apart from M. as a distinct document, the arrangement of the materials appears perplexing with only sporadic coherence. But, considered as a unit-by-unit commentary to, and supplement of, M., T. appears as a well-constructed and orderly document.

Tosefta cannot be fully understood apart from M. because M. provides the entire underlying organizational structure of T. Accordingly, it is imperative then to consider T.'s relationship to M. as a whole to see how its redactor organized the materials according to M.'s sequence. Also it is important to distinguish the two types of materials which T. appends to M.–(1) comments on M.'s materials, and (2) autonomous traditions embedded in T. In conjunction with this latter concern, it is helpful to analyze the literary traits of T., its forms and formulary patterns.

First of all, the organization of T.'s chapters tells us how what the redactor of T. understood the organization of M. itself. T.'s six (E.: seven) chapters relate to M. as follows.

Chapter one of T. corresponds to chapter one of M. But the first pericope of T.'s chapter two supplements M. 1:5. This pericope is not tightly integral to M. chapter one. T. links it to the traditions which follow at M. 2:1.

T. chapter two links chapters two and three of M. together by including together the traditions which relate to these two M. chapters in a single T.-chapter. Thus T. sees the concern of M. 2:5-8 continuing in M. 3:1 and joins the materials of the chapters accordingly.

T.'s chapter three corresponds to M. chapters four and five.

Likewise T. chapter four corresponds to M. chapter six.

T. chapter five is a bit more complex. It opens with autonomous supplements to M. chapter six (T. 5:1-13). The remainder of the chapter then closely corresponds to chapters seven and eight of M. As I said, the Erfurt manuscript gives T. 5:25-32 as a separate chapter. Thus it follows more finely the internal divisions of M.

Finally, T. chapter six, in its entirety, corresponds to M. chapter nine, the last unit of the tractate.

With several exceptions, T. orders its materials in these larger units to follow organization of the individual pericopae of M. These exceptions are as follows:

T. 3:8, corresponds best to M.8:8. But T. links it with T. 3:7 and places it in the context of materials relevant to M. chapter four.

T. 5:21 should better be juxtaposed with M. 8:8 as well. For, both relate to the response "Amen" to blessings. But T. uses it to conclude the materials which correspond to chapter seven of M. Perhaps T., as M., sees this pericope, though independent of its context, as a fitting conclusion for a larger unit of materials.

Three other pericope lack a proper context as they presently stand–T.5:22-24. T.'s redactor puts them between the materials for chapters seven and eight. It is possible to locate 5:22-3 in the context of M. 9:3, and 5:23 in the context of M. 6:8.

Oddly, T. places five pericopae which supplement M. 5:2 between its traditions which correspond to M. 4:4 and M. 4:5. T. appears to "revise" M.'s organization at this juncture.

Apparently T. also varies its view of the internal order of M.'s chapters in two other cases. It gives a pericope corresponding to M. 7:2 after its supplement to M. 7:4, and it presents the exegesis relevant to M. 9:5 before the materials for M. 9:3. Otherwise T. carefully and systematically adheres to the order and organization of M.

Last, T. presents relevant comments or supplements for all but seven M. pericopae: M. 3:6, M. 4:7, M. 5:3-5, M. 7:5, and M. 8:7.

Table I

The chart which follows shows the correspondence between Tosefta and Mishnah for each pericope.

T.	M.	T.	M.	T.	M.
1:1	1:1	3:11	5:2	5:13	6:6
1:2	1:2	3:12	5:2	5:14	7:1-2
1:3	1:3	3:13	5:2	5:15	7:1-2
1:4	1:3	3:14	4:5-6	5:16	7:1-2
1:5	1:4	3:16	4:5-6	5:17	7:1-2
1:6	1:4	3:17	4:5-6	5:18A-C	7:1-2
1:7	1:4	3:18	4:5-6	5:18D-E	7:3
1:8	1:4	3:19	4:5-6	5:19	7:4
1:9	1:4	—	4:7	5:20	7:2
1:10	1:5	3:20	5:1	—	7:5
1:11	1:5	3:21	5:1	5:21	8:8
1:12	1:5	3:22	5:1	5:22	9:3
1:13	1:5	3:23	5:2	5:23	9:3
1:14	1:5	3:24	5:2	5:24	6:8
1:15	1:5	3:25	5:2	5:25	8:1
2:1	1:5	—	5:3-5	5:26	8:2
2:2	2:1	3:26	(8:8)	5:27	8:3
—	2:2	4:1	6:1-3	5:28	8:4
2:3	2:3	4:2	6:1-3	5:29	8:4
2:4	2:3	4:3	6:1-3	5:30	8:5
2:5	2:3	4:4	6:1-3	5:31	8:6
2:6	2:4	4:5	6:1-3	5:32	8:6
2:7	2:4	4:7	6:1-3	—	8:7
2:8	2:4	4:8	6:4-6	6:19	9:5
2:9	2:4	4:9	6:4-6	6:1	9:1-2
2:10	2:5-8	4:10	6:4-6	6:2	9:1-2
2:11	3:1-2	4:11	6:4-6	6:3	9:1-2
—	3:3	4:12	6:4-6	6:4	9:1-2
2:12	3:4	4:13	6:7	6:5	9:1-2
2:13	3:4	4:14	6:7	6:6	9:1-2
2:14	3:5	4:15A-N	6:7	6:7A-F	9:5
2:15	3:5	4:15O-DD	6:8	6:7G-J	9:3
2:16	3:5	4:16	6:8	6:8	9:3
2:17	3:5	4:17	6:8	6:9	9:3
2:18	3:5	4:18	6:8	6:10	9:3
2:19	3:5	4:19	6:8	6:11	9:3
2:20	3:5	4:20	6:8	6:12	9:3
2:21	3:5	4:21	6:8	6:13	9:3
—	3:6	5:1	6:8	6:14	9:3
3:1	4:1	5:2	6:8	6:15	9:4
3:2	4:1	5:3	6:8	6:16	9:4
3:3A	4:1	5:4	6:8	6:17	9:4
3:3B-F	4:2-3	5:5	6:6	6:18	9:4
3:4	4:2-3	5:6	6:6	6:20	9:5
3:5	4:2-3	5:7	6:6	6:21	9:5
3:6	4:2-3	5:8	6:6	6:22	9:5
3:7	4:4	5:9	6:6	6:23	9:5
3:8	(8:8)	5:10	6:6	6:24	9:5
3:9	5:2	5:11	6:7		
3:10	5:2	5:12	6:7		

Table II

The correspondence between T. and M.'s chapters is as follows:

T.	M. Chapter
1:1-2:1	1
2:2-10	2
2:11-21	3
3:1-7, 3:14-19	4
3:9-13, 3:20-25	5
5:1-13	6
5:14-21	7
5:25-32	8
6:1-25	9

In order to best describe T.'s relation to M. I presented in chapters 1-9 above the text of each unit of M., along with the relevant texts of T., followed by a brief explanation of the substance of T.'s materials and the relationship between M. and T. Preceding each section I summarize the nature of the material which follows. When one examines the materials of T. in the direct context of M. in this way, one sees the care which T.'s editors exercised in assembling this complicated combination of commentary and supplementary appendix to M.–consisting of a variety of materials including glosses, explanations, expansions, additions and independent excurses on related subjects.

II.   Tosefta's Subdivisions

Let us first summarize in greater detail the overall structure of T. itself. As we have seen T. follows M.'s structure and depends entirely on it for a rational and coherent framework. Internal to T. we find then a great many materials wholly dependent on M. for their meaning. These usually appear together in coherent contiguous groups of pericopae which I here refer to as subdivisions of intermediate divisions. Often, but not always, they cite M. verbatim. In our tractate all told there are eleven such divisions which I describe below (section III).

In our tractate we also find several groups of pericopae which closely correlate to M.'s organization and thematic structure but which, in addition, have coherent themes of their own and independent formulary traits. I list six such units in section IV. I find also one division which complements M. and bears common formulary patterns but no real cogent theme, which I also describe in section IV.

Finally, I analyze in section V thirteen intermediate divisions which supplement M. and are fully independent of M.'s structure and content. Ten of these units exhibit two sorts of formal and thematic coherence: six show internally unitary formulary traits and take up coherent issues. Four divisions have externally unitary formulary traits and deal with coherent themes. The three remaining independent divisions include two which develop a cogent theme but show no marked formulary coherence and one remaining unit which exhibits neither formulary nor thematic cogency. This latter item is defined by the units which bound it before and after as a separate subdivision of T. The catalogue which follows describes then each intermediate division of T. Berakhot as I have outlined.

III.   Intermediate Divisions Wholly Dependent on Mishnah

The eleven subdivisions included here depend on Mishnah for their structure, coherence and continuity.   An intermediate division is wholly dependent on Mishnah in one of two ways. First it may cite and gloss Mishnah's pericopae in a sequential fashion.   Second it may string together individual and disjoint pericopae in such away that it is clear that the redactor of T. assembles the unit to follow M.'s organization to gloss or elucidate M. by juxtaposing materials to M. but without citing M. If a sequence of two or more pericopae which form an intermediate division is intelligible apart from M. but serves to complement M. we generally include it on the next list (IV). But if the sequence appears in the context of a long subdivision organized tightly around M.'s structure, it is included herewith.

1. T. 1:1-15. T. cites M. four times and adds materials to augment and clarify M. T. 1:1 cites and supplements M. 1:1. T. 1:2 cites and glosses M. 1:2 and illustrates it with a story. T. 1:3 gives a contrasting exegesis for the verse of M. 1:3. T. 1:4 has a story to illustrate M. 1:3. T. 1:5 cites and augments the list of M. 1:4. T. 1:6-9 lists the blessings alluded to in M. and in T.'s preceding gloss to M. T. 1:10 opens with a citation of M.1:5 and carries it forward in a long unit. Much of the material is incomprehensible outside its juxtaposition with M. (T. 1:2D-H, 3, 4, 6-9, 10-15). But M. serves as the framework for the construction of the chapter. The unit in T. does not develop its own conceptions, or work out new issues, or utilize a coherent formulary pattern. As I said, it systematically presents materials which elucidate, or expand upon, M. The glosses and explanations of M. are given as simple declarative sentences, two disputes (1:1), two stories (1:2D-H), a long well-patterned list with interpolations (1:6-9), and two exegetical units, one short(1:3) and one long (1:10-15). As noted, the unit has no pervasive coherent formulary pattern.

2. T. 2:10-13. T. 2:10 uses the contrastive predicate verbs of M. 2:5-3:3, exempt/obligated, as it augments M. 2:5A. T. 2:11 cites M. 3:2 and augments. Judah's expansion follows M.'s sentence construction. T. 2:10J-K raises one of T.'s own issues, i.e. whether one interrupts activity to say the *Shema* or the Prayer, cf. T. 2:6 above. T. 2:12 augments M. 3:4A with its own issue. But T. 2:13 returns to rework M. 3:4A directly and add to it a story. Declarative sentences are employed throughout.

3. **T. 3:1-5.** T. 3:1-2 systematically cite and gloss M. 4:1. T.3:2A alludes to M. 4:1. T. 3:3B echoes M. 4:3C and then adds to it. T. 3:4 continues T. 3:3. T. 3:5 appends another Aqiba-tradition. T. 3:3B-3:4D are two sets of two balanced contrasting sentences.

4. **T. 3:7-9.** This may be a continuation of the division begun at no. 3 immediately above. T. 3:6 then is a lengthy exegetical digression within the unit. T. 3:7A cites M. 4:4 and glosses. T.3:7G-H is related and carries T. 3:8 in its wake. 3:8 is unitary in form and independent in substance. We choose to include it here because it intrudes into another division wholly dependent on M. for its redactional structure and does not stand on its own as a significant intermediate division. T. 3:9 glosses M. 5:2.

5. **T. 3:18-22.** The unit follows M.'s structure which wholly determines its organization. T. 3:18 cites and glosses M. 4:5A. T. 3:19D augments M. 4:6, the wagon or boat. T. 3:20 augments M.5:1D-E first with a new ruling then with an illustrative story. T. 3:21 cites and glosses M. 5:1A. T. 3:22 supplies a new context for M. 5:1D.

6. **T. 4:12.** T. cites M. 6:6C and glosses. This leads then to a complementary unit which follows on the list below, section iv.D.1.

7. **T. 5:18-20.** T. 5:18A-C augments M. 7:2. T. 5:18D-E glosses M. 7:3. T. 5:19 concludes M. 7:4. T. 5:20 adds new material on the issue of the chapter.

8. **T. 5:25-32.** The correspondence is as follows: T. 5:25 to M.8:1, T. 5:26 to M. 8:2, T. 5:27 to M. 8:3, T. 5:28 to M. 8:4. T. cites M. and glosses in each case. T. 5:29 augments with another dispute. T. 5:30 revises M. 8:5, then augments. T. 5:31A-D alludes to M. 8:6D, and F-G to M. 8:6A. The rest augments M.

9. **T. 6:2-6.** T. 6:2B cites M. 9:1B and expands. The protasis "one who sees" recurs throughout: T. 6:2A, D, 6:3A, 6:5A, 6:6B. At 6:6D Judah glosses his ruling found at M. 9:2C-D. T. 6:2 uses long balanced full declarative sentences. We place the unit on this list because it opens and closes with citation of or allusion to M. 9:1 and 9:2 respectively. It is dependent on M. for its organization.

10. **T. 6:7-8.** T. 6:7A-F parallels M. 9:5A-F. T. 6-7G-H glosses M. 9:3C-D. T. 6:8 continues T. 6:7. One might argue that this division continues the above.

11. **T. 6:16-24E.** T. 6:16 cites M. 9:4 and expands. T. 6:17 further augments. T. 6:19 cites and glosses M. 9:5G-J. T. 6:21 cites and glosses M.

9:5K-M. T. 6:22 augments. T. 6:23 cites and supplies a context for M. 9:5O-R and T. 6:24A-E supplies a context for M. 9:5R. T. 6:18 and 6:20 augment.

(T. 3:26. This singleton repeats M. 8:8.)

(T. 5:21. Cf. M. 8:8. This goes together with 5:22-24 as a group lacking coherent theme and form in the list below.)

IV. Complements to Mishnah.
Intermediate Divisions Correlated to M. but Formulated Independent of M.

A. [No intermediate division which complements M. in our tractate bears both internally unitary formulary traits and coherent themes.]

B. **Externally Unitary Formulary Traits and Coherent Themes**

1. **T. 2:1-5.** Closely, but not wholly, correlated to M. Declarative sentences throughout. The first two pericopae complement M. 1:5 and 2:1 respectively. T. 2:1 augments M. 1:5A with closely related rulings. T. 2:2 gives a general principle which stands behind M. 2:1A and then augments a new ruling. T. 2:3A cites M. 2:3F and augments. T. 2:5 alludes to M. 2:3G and carries it forward in detail. So too for T. 2:5. The subdivision has its own external formulary coherence. "He who recites the *Shema*" opens each pericope. "And so too concerning..." recurs at T.2:3B, 2:4C, 2:4G. "He should not return" at T. 2:4A and 2:4E contrast with "he should return" at T. 2:5A, 2:5B and 2:5C.

2. **T. 2:6-9.** This complementary unit relates to M. 2:4 but is not dependent on it. The issue of T. 2:6 is new but augments M.'s concern with special rulings for various professions. T. 2:7 complements M. 2:4. T. 2:8 draws on M. 2:4 for one phrase and augments it. T. 2:9 carries M. 2:4 forward on a related issue. The formulary pattern of the sentences is repeated as are the phrases: "Those who write," "The porter," "Workers," "The attendants," respectively precede "interrupt to recite," "...recites," "may recite." The sentences are balanced and T. 2:7 and 2:8 form a somewhat balanced pair of sets of sentences. 2:9 is a nicely formulated list with present participle verbs, perhaps a continuation of 2:6–"recite," "bless," "eat," "bless," "pray," "but may not go down." 2:9 continues but does not cite M. 2:4.

3. **T. 2:14-15.** T. complements M. 3:5E-I. T. continues the above complementary section, T. 2:6-9. "Behold he may recite...in any case one should not pray" (T. 2:14H-I – cf. T. 2:7A, D, 2:8C.) T. 2:15B, E, also echo "behold it is permissible."

4. **T. 2:16-21.** T. complements M. 3:5J-L. 2:16G, H, I are nicely balanced with the phrases "recite/not recite." 2:17-19 are straightforward. 2:20 is a long well-constructed unit. 2:21 gives a set of three pairs of lemmas with

an appropriate verse. No internal unitary formulary structure. In fact, 2:20-21 could stand as independent supplements. But they complement M.'s concern as they deal with its issue, recitation when not clothed.

5. T. 3:14-17. T. 3:14 augments M. 4:5-6. T. 3:15-16, a ladder, generalizes the rules of M. 4:5-6. T. 3:17 concludes the supplement. A verse follows each ruling: 3:14B, 3:15B, 3:16B, D, 3:17C to round out the externally unitary formulary pattern on the coherent theme.

6. T. 4:3-5. T. 4:3 expands M. 6:1D. T. 4:4A-C adds to M. 6:1. T. 4:4D cites M. 6:1H and gives another version of Judah's gloss. T. 4:4F trails T. 4:5 in its wake. The displaced object of the preposition serves as protasis for the sentences which spell out the dispute at T. 4:3. The forms follow the function of the unit. That is, they allow blessings to be prescribed for each specific food. Longer and fuller sentences comprise T. 4:4F-4:5.

C. [No divisions complementary to M. present cogent themes without any formulary coherence.]

D.   Formal Coherence but No Cogent Theme

1. T. 4:13-18. T. 4:13-4:15N augment M. 6:7. T. 4:15A-N has a list of five cases. T. 4:15 O-DD revises the dispute of M. 6:8. T. 4:16 cites M. 6:8G-H in the context of a lengthy story. T.4:18, another story, continues T. 4:17's concerns.

V.   Supplements to M.   Intermediate Divisions Independent of M.

A. Internally Unitary Formulary Traits and Coherent Themes

1. T. 3:6. This singleton is a lengthy exegetical pericope which intrudes on an intermediate division wholly dependent on M. The pericope repeats its pattern five times: "Lest one think..." + citation of verse. It is internally unitary in form and substance.

2. T. 4:6-7. T. has its own concerns – the change of blessing as one prepares the food for eating, and the blessing after eating. The perfectly balanced units of choppy sentences conclude with the longer general rules of 4:6F-G. The issue commences again at T. 4:15 (see above iv.D.1).

3. T. 4:19-5:4. Deals with blessings required because of interruptions in the meal. The form is tight and repetitive. 4:19-21 cohere in theme and display internally unitary formal structure. 5:1-4 are coherent in theme and bear externally unitary formal structure and might best be classed on the following list below (V.B.3).

4. T. 5:14-17. T. apparently augments M. 7:1-2. But in fact, T. is interested in an entirely different issue – the obligation for reciting the blessing after the meal, rather than the invitation to recite the blessing. It is comprised of a well-balanced sequence with a list of ten followed by a gloss (5:17C). This unit would make a fine segment of a chapter in M.

5. T. 6:1. Long independent pericope which provides an exegetical introduction to the chapter. Tight construction but a candidate for the following list (V.B).

6. T. 6:9-15. T. raises new concerns of its own. The long well-constructed unit repeats "one who...says" throughout. 6:15 concludes the section with a new tightly formulated issue.

B. Externally Unitary Formulary Traits and Coherent Themes

1. T. 3:23-25. These pericopae deal with the particulars of the text of the prayer. 3:23-24 are apocopated and well-balanced. But 3:25 starts on another issue before returning to the form and general concern of 3:24 – "He includes...."

2. T. 4:8 -11. T. is interested in laws for the dinner, not in rules concerning blessings. Balanced declarative sentences convey the rules.

3. T. 4:19-5:4. See above list V.A.3.

4. T. 5:5-13. T. gives rules for the dinner. 5:5-7 use apocopated or simple sentences, balanced with care. 5:8-9 are a set of two rules – "One should not...." 5:11, 12, 13 stand apart from the preceding and from each other. All deal with the dinner. In a broad sense we have here a coherent theme.

C. Cogent Theme, No Formulary Coherence

1. T. 3:10-13. T. develops its own concerns in a balanced unit. It relates slightly to the issue of insertions into the prayer raised at M. 5:2. In 3:10-11 the sentences are apocopated and the pattern repeats: protasis, illustrations, ruling, gloss for not saying. 3:12-13 raise related issues using new forms (e.g. Houses' disputes). There is no unity of form if the unit is considered as one division. But the issues are cogent.

2. T. 4:1-2. T. 4:1 introduces the subdivision followed by 4:2 (see Lieberman, cited above). The unit is distinguished by a lack of unitary form and questionable thematic coherence. Nonetheless it precedes the complements to M. 6:1 and follows the supplements to M. 5:2. The forms vary too much to be considered consistent – "One should not...," "he who," list + "one recites..."

D. [No divisions exhibit formal coherence without thematic cogency.]

E. No Thematic Cogency or Formulary Coherence

1. T. 5:21-24. Bounded on both sides by divisions wholly dependent on M. Cf. M. 8:8, T. 6:14-15. Miscellanies.

VI. Summary

The last group of T.'s units, those thirteen supplements independent of M. (40% of T.'s subdivisions) generally take up issues or conceptions not explored in M. The best of these units could constitute fine additional chapters of M. At the very least the existence of such divisions highlights the foci and thematic choices of M. They show which competing issues could have been addressed by M. but were not. The remaining eighteen intermediate divisions (60% of T.'s divisions) serve as the first level of commentary to M. Much of this Toseftan material finds its way into the later rabbinic discussions of M. in the Talmuds Babli and Yerushalmi.

Table III

The chart which follows summarizes our observations regarding the breakdown of T.'s divisions.

Intermediate divisions of T.: Wholly dependent on M (a), Complements (b), and Supplements (c).

	a.	b.	c.
1.	T. 1:1-15		
2.		T. 2:1-5	
3.		T. 2:6-9	
4.	T. 2:10-13		
5.		T. 2:14-15	
6.		T. 2:16-21	
7.	T. 3:1-5		
8.			T. 3:6
9.	T. 3:7-9		
10.			T.3:10-13
11.		T. 3:14-17	
12.	T. 3:18-19		
13.	T. 3:20-22		
14.			T. 3:23-25
(14a)	(T. 3:26)		
15.			T. 4:1-2
16.		T. 4:3-5	
17.			T. 4:6-7
18.			T. 4:8-11
(18a)	T. 4:12		
19.		T. 4:13-18	
20.			T. 4:19-5:4
21.			T. 5:5-13
22.			T. 5:14-17
23.	T. 5:18-20		
(23a)	(T. 5:21)		
24.			T. 5:22-23
(24a)			T. 5:24
25.	T. 5:25-32		
26.			T. 6:1
27.	T. 6:2-6		
28.	T. 6:7-8		
29.			T. 6:9-15
30.	T. 6:16-24E		
31.			T. 6:24F-25

Figure 1

Mishnah's Phenomenology of Prayer

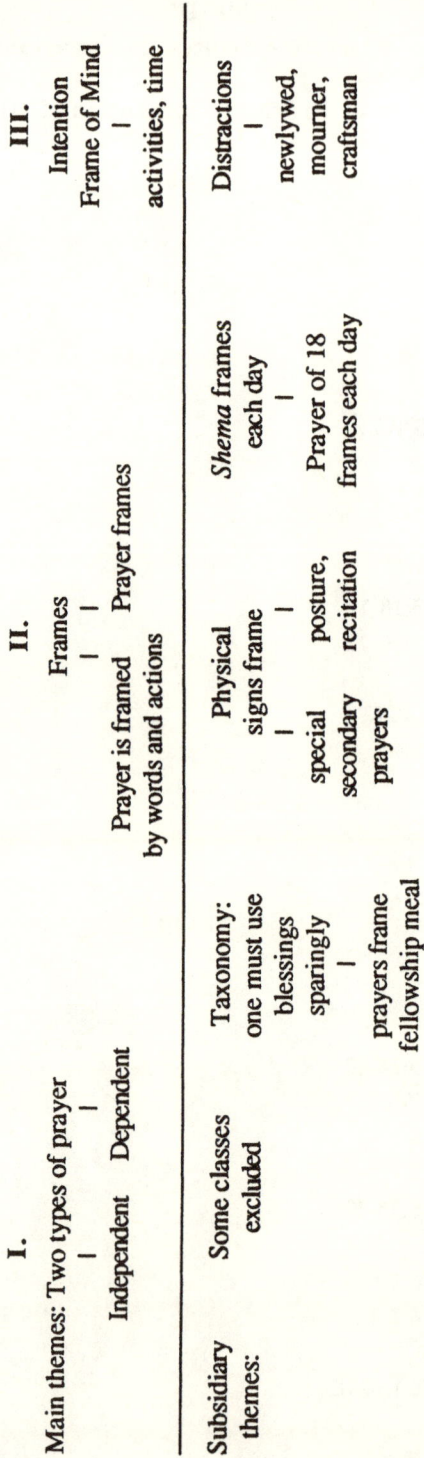

	I.	II.	III.
Main themes:	Two types of prayer — Independent Dependent	Frames — Prayer is framed Prayer frames by words and actions	Intention Frame of Mind — activities, time
Subsidiary themes:	Some classes excluded	Taxonomy: one must use blessings sparingly — prayers frame fellowship meal	Physical signs frame — special secondary prayers	posture, recitation	*Shema* frames each day — Prayer of 18 frames each day	Distractions — newlywed, mourner, craftsman

Abbreviations

I. General

Albeq = Hanok Albeq, *Shishah Sidre Mishnah*, vols. I-VI, Jer., 1952-1959.

ARN = Abot deRabbi Nathan

B. = Babli, Babylonian Talmud

Ber. = Berakhot

B.R. = Bereshit Rabbah

Danby = Herbert Danby, *The Mishnah: Translated from the Hebrew with Introduction and brief explanatory notes,* London, 1933.

Deut. = Deuteronomy

Douglas, Natural Symbols = Mary Douglas, *Natural Symbols: Explorations in Cosmology,* N.Y., 1973.

Douglas, Purity and Danger = Mary Douglas, *Purity and Danger: An Analysis of Concepts of Pollution and Taboo,* London, 1966.

D.R. = Defus Rishon: First printed edition of T., Venice, 1521.

E. = Erfurt MSS of T.

Eleazar = Tzvee Zahavy, *The Traditions of Eleazar Ben Azariah,* Missoula, 1977.

Ezek. = Ezekiel

Gen. = Genesis

Gereboff, Tarfon = Joel Gereboff, *The Traditions of Tarfon,* Missoula, 1979.

GRA = Elijah b. Solomon Zalman (1720-1797) commentary of, from M. ed. Romm.

Hasde David = David Pardo, *Sefer Hasde David.*

Heinemann, Prayer = Joseph Heinemann, *Prayer in the Talmud: Forms and Patterns.* English ed. by R. S. Sarason, Berlin, 1977.

Hertz = Joseph H. Hertz, *The Authorized Daily Prayer Book,* N. Y., 1974.

Isa. = Isaiah

Jastrow = Marcus Jastrow, *A Dictionary of the Targumim, The Talmud Babli and Yerushalmi and Midrashic Literature,* N.Y., 1971.

Lev. = Leviticus

Lieberman = Saul Lieberman, ed., *The Tosefta: Zera'im,* N.Y., 1955.

lit. = literally

Lukyn-Williams = A. Lukyn-Williams, *Tractate Berakoth: Mishna and Tosephta*, N.Y., 1921.

M. = Mishnah

Meg. = Megillah

MSS = Manuscript

Mu. = Babylonian Talmud: Codex Munich, reprint Jer., 1971.

Neh. = Nehemiah

Neusner, HMLP = Jacob Neusner, *A History of the Mishnaic Law of Purities*, Leiden, 1974-1977.

Neusner, Invitation = Jacob Neusner, *Invitation to the Talmud*, N. Y., 1973.

Pes. = Pesahim

Qoh. = Qohelet

Sacks = Nissan Sacks, ed., *The Mishnah with Variant Readings, Mishnah Zera'im*, Volume one, Jer., 1972.

Sem. = Semahot

Seride HaYerushalmi = L. Ginzberg, *Yerushalmi Fragments from the Genizah*, N.Y., 1909.

Shab. = Shabbat

Sot. = Sotah

T. = Tosefta

TK = Saul Lieberman, *Tosefta Ki-fshutah: A Comprehensive Commentary on the Tosefta*, part I, N.Y., 1955.

Var. = Variant reading

W. = Vienna MSS of T.

Y. = Yerushalmi

Zeb. = Zebahim

IQSa = Serekh Ha-Edah in Jacob Licht, ed., *Manual of Discipline*, Jerusalem, 1961.

II. Journals

HTR	Harvard Theological Review
JBL	Journal of Biblical Literature
JJS	Journal of Jewish Studies
JQR	Jewish Quarterly Review
MGWJ	Monatsschrift fur Geschichte und Wissenschaft des Judentums
PAAJR	Proceedings of American Academy for Jewish Research
REJ	Revue des Etudes Juifs

RQ   Revue de Qumran

Selected Bibliography

Albeq, Hanok. *Shishah Sidre Mishnah*. Vols. I-VI. Jerusalem: 1952-1959.

Babylonian Talmud: Codex Munich. Reprint Jerusalem: 1971.

Barthelemy, D., and Milik, J. T., eds. *Discoveries in the Judean Desert I. Qumran Cave I*. Oxford: 1955.

Bickermann, Elias J. "The Civic Prayer for Jerusalem." *HTR*. Vol. LV. No. 3. July, 1962. Pp. 163-185.

Bokser, Baruch. "Philo's Description of Jewish Practices." *Protocols of the Center for Hermeneutical Studies in Hellenistic and Modern Cultures*. Berkeley: 1977.

Carmignac, J., Cothenet, E., and Lignee, H., eds. *Les Textes de Qumran II*. Paris: 1963.

Carmignac, J., and Guilbert, P., eds. *Les Textes de Qumran I*. Paris: 1961.

Danby, Herbert. *The Mishnah: Translated from the Hebrew with Introduction and Brief Explanatory Notes*. London: 1933.

Derovan, David, ed. *Prayer: A Study Guide to the Philosophy and Meaning of Tefilah*. Yavneh Studies. Vol. 3. N.Y.: 1970.

Douglas, Mary. *Implicit Meanings: Essays in Anthropology*. London: 1975.

Douglas, Mary. *Natural Symbols: Explorations in Cosmology*. N.Y.: 1973.

Douglas, Mary. *Purity and Danger: An Analysis of Concepts of Pollution and Taboo*. London: 1966.

Droshkewicz, A., ed. *Novellae and Explanations of Elijah Ben Solomon (GRA) on Tractate Berakhot*. Reprint Jerusalem: 1973.

Eisenstadt, S. N., ed. *Intellectuals and Tradition*. Jerusalem: 1973.

Elbogen, Ismar. *The Historical Development of Jewish Prayer*. Revised Hebrew version by J. Heinemann. Jerusalem: 1972.

Finkelstein, Louis. "The *Birkat ha-Mazon*." *JQR* N.S. XIX. 1928-9. Pp. 211-262.

Flusser, D. "Qumran and Jewish Apotropaic Prayers." *IEJ*. 16., 1966. Pp. 194-205.

Gartner, Bertil. *The Temple and the Community in Qumran and the New Testament*. Cambridge: 1965.

Gereboff, Joel. *The Traditions of Tarfon*. Missoula: 1979.

Ginzberg, L. *Yerushalmi Fragments from the Genizah.* Reprint Jerusalem: 1968.

Goldschmidt, E. D. *On Jewish Liturgy: Essays on Prayer and Religious Poetry.* Jerusalem: 1978.

Goody, Jack. *The Domestication of the Savage Mind.* Cambridge: 1977.

Harrelson, Walter. *From Fertility Cult to Worship.* N.Y.: 1969.

Heiler, Fredrich. *Prayer. A Study in the History and Psychology of Religion.* London: 1932.

Heinemann, Joseph. *"Birkat Ha-Zimmun and Havurah Meals."* JJS.   Vol. 13. 1962. Pp. 23-29.

Heinemann, Joseph. "The Formula *melekh ha-olam."* JJS. Vol. XI. Nos. 3-4. 1960. Pp. 177-179.

Heinemann, Joseph. "Once Again *melekh ha-olam."* JJS. Vol. XV. Nos. 3-4. 1964. Pp. 149-154.

Heinemann, Joseph. *Prayer in the Talmud: Forms and Patterns.* English version by R. S. Sarason. Berlin: 1977.

Hershler, M., ed. *Ginze Rishonim. Berakhot.* Jerusalem: 1967.

Hertz, Joseph H. *The Authorized Daily Prayer Book.* N.Y.: 1974.

Howard, George. "The Tetragram and the New Testament." *JBL.* Vol. 96, No. 1, 1977. Pp. 63-83.

Idelson, A. Z. *Jewish Liturgy and Its Development.* N.Y.: 1932.

Jastrow, Marcus. *A Dictionary of the Targumim, the Tabmud Babli and Yerushalmi, and Midiashic Literature.* Repr. N. Y.: 1971.

Jay, E. G. *Origen's Treatise on Prayer.* London: 1954.

Jeremias, Joachim. *The Prayers of Jesus.* Phila.: 1978.

Katsh, Abraham. "Tractate Berakhot from the Genizah." Hebrew. In *Sefer Shazar,* Jerusalem: 1973.

Krauss, Samuel. *Synagogale Altertumer.* Hildesheim: 1966.

Leach, Edmund. *Culture and Communication: The Logic by Which Symbols are Connected.* Cambridge: 1976.

Leaney, A. R. C. *The Rule of Qumran and Its Meaning.* London: 1966.

Licht, Jacob, ed. *Megillat HaHodayoth.* Jerusalem: 1957.

Licht, Jacob, ed. *Megillat HaSerakhim.* Jerusalem: 1965.

Lieberman, Saul, ed. *Baron Jubilee Volume.* Vols. I, II. N.Y.: 1974.

Lieberman, Saul. "Light on the Cave Scrolls from Rabbinic Sources." *PAAJR.* Vol. XX. 1951. Pp. 395-404.

Lieberman, Saul. *The Tosefta: Zera'im.* N.Y.: 1955.

Lieberman, Saul. *Tosefta Ki-fshutah: A Comprehensive Commentary on the Tosefta.* Part I. N.Y.: 1955.

Leibreich, L. J. "The Benediction Immediately Preceding and the One Following the Recital of the *Shema." REJ.* CXXV. 1966. Pp. 151-165.

Liber, Maurice. "La Recitation des *Schema* et des Benedictions." *REJ.* LVII. Pp. 161-193; LVIII. Pp. 1-22.

Liber, Maurice. "The Structure and History of the Tefillah." *JQR.* N.S. LV. 1949-50. Pp. 331-357.

Lohse, E., and Schlichting, G., eds. *Die Tosefta. Text, Ubersetzung und Erklarung. Seder Zera'im.* Heft 1-3. Kohlhammer: 1956-1958.

Lukyn-Williams, A. *Tractate Berakoth: Mishna and Tosefta.* N.Y.: 1921.

Marcus, R. "Divine Names and Attributes in the Septuagint." *PAAJR.* 1931/2, 1932, 3-120.

Millgram, A. *Jewish Worship.* Phila.: 1971.

Munk, Eli. *The World of Prayers.* Vol. I. Hebrew. Jerusalem: 1974.

Neusner, Jacob. *A History of the Mishnaic Law of Purities.* Vols. I-XXII. Leiden: 1974-1977.

Neusner, Jacob. *Invitation to the Talmud.* N.Y.: 1973.

Neusner, Jacob. *The Tosefta in English. Sixth Division. Tohoroth.* N.Y.: 1977.

Oppenheimer, Aharon. *The Am Ha-Aretz.* Leiden: 1977.

Petuchowski, J. J., ed. *Contributions to the Scientific Study of Jewish Liturgy.* N. Y.: 1970.

Priesendanz, K. *Papyri Graecae Magicae.* Vols. I, II. Berlin: 1928.

Roth, Cecil. "*Melekh ha-olam:* Zealot Influence in the Liturgy?" JJS. Vol. XI. Nos. 3-4. 1960. Pp. 173-175.

Rowley, H. H. *Worship in Ancient Israel: Its Forms and Meaning.* London: 1967.

Sacks, Y. L., ed. *Commentary of Elijah of London.* Jerusalem: 1956.

Sacks, Nissan. *The Mishnah with Variant Readings. Order Zera'im (I).* Jerusalem: 1972.

Sacks, Nissan, ed. *Tosafot Rabennu Yehudah Sirleon. Berakhot.* Vol. I. Jerusalem: 1969.

Sanders, J. A. *The Dead Sea Psalms Scroll.* Ithaca: 1967.

Schwab, Moses, ed. *The Talmud of Jerusalem.* Vol. I. Berakhoth. Reprint N.Y.: 1969.

Smith, Morton. *Jesus the Magician.* N.Y.: 1978.

Spanier, A. *"Die erste Benediktion des achtzehngebetes."* *MGWJ.* Vol. 81. 1937. Pp. 714-716.

Stendahl, Krister, ed. *The Scrolls and the New Testament.* N.Y.: 1957.

Sutcliffe, E. F. "Sacred Meals at Qumran?" *Heythrop Journal.* Vol. I, 1960. Pp. 48-65.

Talmon, S. "The Manual of Benedictions of the Sect of the Judean Desert." *RQ.* Vol. 2. 1960. Pp. 475-500.

Tambiah, S. J. "The Magical Power of Words." *Man.* Vol. 3. 1968. Pp. 175-208.

Underhill, Evelyn. *Worship.* N.Y.: 1957.

Vermes, Geza. *The Dead Sea Scrolls in English.* London: 1970.

Weisenberg, E. J. "The Liturgical Term *Melekh ha-olam."* *JJS.* Vol. XV. Nos. 1-2. 1964. Pp. 1-56.

Weiss, J. G. "On the Formula *Melekh ha-olam* as Anti-Gnostic Protest." *JJS.* Vol. X. Nos. 3-4, 1959. Pp. 169-171.

Zahavy, Tzvee. *The Traditions of Eleazar Ben Azariah.* Missoula: 1977.

Zahavy, Tzvee. *The Talmud of the Land of Israel. Tractate Berakhot.* Forthcoming.

Zahavy, Tzvee. *Studies in Early Jewish Prayer.* Studies in Judaism, University Press of America. Lanham, MD: forthcoming.

Zahavy, Tzvee. "The Sabbath Code of Damascus Covenant X, 14-XI, 18: Form Analytical and Redaction Critical Observations." *Revue de Qumran.* Paris: December 1981.

Zahavy, Tzvee. "A New Approach to Early Jewish Prayer." *History of Judaism: the Next Ten Years,* ed. B. Bokser. Brown Judaic Studies 21. Scholars Press, Chico, CA: 1980.

Zahavy, Tzvee. "Sources for the Seasonal Ritual in the Third through Fifth Centuries." *Proceedings of the Ninth World Congress of Jewish Studies.* Jerusalem: 1986.

Zahavy, Tzvee. "Beruryah," "Joshua ben Hananiah," "Judah bar Ilai," "Meir," "Simeon bar Yohai," "Simeon ben Gamaliel," "Tarfon," "Yose ben Halafta." *The Encyclopedia of Religion,* ed. M. Eliade. The Free Press, Macmillan. New York: 1986.

Zahavy, Tzvee. "Concentration for Prayer in the Mishnah and the Talmud," *New Perspectives on Ancient Judaism,* ed. J. Neusner. Lanham, MD: 1987.

Zahavy, Tzvee. "Tosefta Tractate Berakhot," *The Tosefta Translated from the Hebrew. First Division. Zera'im,* ed. J. Neusner. New York: 1986.

Zahavy, Tzvee and Brooks, Roger. "Form Analysis of Mishnaic Sentences." *Computing in the Humanities,* ed. P. Patton. D.C. Heath, Lexington Books: 1981.

Zuckermandel, M. S. *Tosephta: Based on the Erfurt and Vienna Codices.* Reprint Jerusalem: 1970.

Index

www.ingramcontent.com/pod-product-compliance
Lightning Source LLC
Chambersburg PA
CBHW022023090426
42739CB00006BA/266